THE TRUE POWER OF
UNITY

THE TRUE POWER OF
UNITY

BRIAN P. LUCAS

© 2025 by Family Priority Publishing

All rights reserved. No part of this publication may be reproduced, distributed, or transmitted in any form or by any means, including photocopying, recording, or other electronic or mechanical methods, without the prior written permission of the publisher, except in the case of brief quotations embodied in critical reviews and certain other noncommercial uses permitted by copyright law.

All Scripture quotations are from the King James Version of the Bible.

Brian P. Lucas is not a licensed and/or registered rabbi, preacher, bishop, priest, deacon, minister, teacher, theologian, seminary student or attendant, psychologist, therapist, or counselor and is in no way, shape, or form promoting a man-made religion, denomination, or church and/or providing you with any earthly religious advice in any capacity. All subject matter provided herein is for spiritual informational purposes only. Brian P. Lucas does not guarantee you results. You and only you are responsible for what you do or don't do with the spiritual and biblical information provided, so due diligence on your part is an expected and appreciated requirement.

Family Priority Publishing
66 W Flagler St
Suite 900 PMB #10522
Miami, Florida 33130

ISBN:
978-1-7324104-2-8
10 9 8 7 6 5 4 3 2 1

Printed in the United States of America

Lifetime Thanks

To Jan G. Lucas, who believes in me, cares for me, and loves me unconditionally, even when I do not know or understand how to believe in, care for, or love myself — a strong woman who has the eyes to foresee the person I am today, discrediting and contradicting the rest of the world, who told me I would be either in prison or dead by the age of 21. She is a caring woman who has loved me for me from the very beginning, not for what she could get from me, because I can assure you that I had nothing beneficial or productive to give when we met.

Jan sacrificed her time and energy to a lost and hopeless child who was full of pain and bitterness toward the world and everything in it because she could see his potential to become a man with something to offer. She willingly endured the growing pains of a boy as he matured and learned to become the man full of wisdom, knowledge, and power that she always knew was within.

Jan is an independent and self-sufficient woman who refuses to settle for less or accept mediocrity, no matter the circumstances, with or without the approval of others; a natural-born leader who understands the importance of being quick to hear and slow to speak; a silent but deadly opponent at the snap of a finger; an empowering and encouraging woman who always reminds me to use the negatives from my past to create a better future and tells me that the greatest way to silence the doubters and naysayers is simply to succeed.

Jan is a soldier, always hands-on, never sitting on the sidelines. She is a true representation of the support any real man needs to stay focused and continue to push forward through each phase of life. Jan says what she means and means what she says.

She loves and trusts God and is a true representation of who and what she believes in, even till her death.

Jan brings light to the dark, smiles to the sad, joy to the brokenhearted, love to the hurt, strength to the weak, and hope to the hopeless; to say she has a strong work ethic, excellent morals, great character, and a magnetic and cheerful attitude would be an understatement.

Jan is the most Christ-like of anyone I have ever encountered in my life, a true woman of God who is full of faith and walks what she talks!

Jan, I need you to know that I love you, I miss you, and I am eternally grateful for every investment you made into my life that has undisputedly played a major role in making me the man I am today.

I will always love you, Jan, and I will see you again.

Brian P. Lucas

BRIAN P. LUCAS

Dedication

I dedicate this book to every one of you who has invested your time and energy into reading it and is seriously interested in implementing the changes required to be the best you that you desire to be and to be all that God has ordained and sanctified you to be.

Congratulations on taking a step forward toward improvement for yourself and your family and allowing me to be a part of your journey.

I wish you the very best to truly succeed in all your endeavors, and I encourage you to keep reading books, learning new things, and exposing yourself to experiences that challenge you to make sacrifices and implement changes that ultimately promote elevation, growth, and development.

I strongly encourage you to use this time as an investment with the hopes of achieving a huge return. To do so, you will need to eliminate any distractions and make reading, studying, and comprehending each chapter of this book a priority.

Thank you for granting me permission to speak into your life. I assure you that I will be 100 percent real with you on all levels; I will be very blunt, holding nothing back and telling it just like it is through the duration of the book.

I look forward to your success as you take this journey one chapter at a time.

To Finding The True Power of Unity within,

Brian P. Lucas
BRIAN P. LUCAS

Table of Contents

Lifetime Thanks v
Dedication vii
Foreword xi
Introduction xii
Chapter 1: Unity Begins with U 1
Chapter 2: Unity Eliminates Lack 13
Chapter 3: The Enemy of Unity 27
Chapter 4: Beware of Prideful Unity 37
Chapter 5: Destructive Unity 49
Appendix: Divide to Conquer 55
Bonus Chapter: Purpose to Impact 63
Conclusion 97
Why Jesus 100
Salvation 101
About the Author 103

Foreword

Brian P. Lucas has the unique ability to search out and bring forth the practical meaning of the spiritual truth of unity, and to carefully remove the exterior covering of the cliches that obscure reality.

Brian has done it time and again and has surely opened my eyes and the eyes of many and will surely open something in you that you have never seen before.

This book will unlock steps of walking in unity and take the mystery out of your success in life matters, if you are trapped in a mundane and mediocre existence.

Brian's insights are the perfect prescription to inject a new outlook on life.

It is a fact that, in creation, when unity is applied, all things are possible.

The greatest tragedy in life is not death, it is the lack of understanding *The True Power of Unity*.

May the following pages stir in your spirit the inspiration, motivation, and passion to complete your God-given purpose and move you daily from glory to glory.

Minister Dane Brown

Introduction

There is no *unity* that outweighs, outperforms, or outlasts *The True Power of Unity*.

The perfect definition for *The True Power of Unity* is:

1. God the Father.
2. God the Son.
3. God the Holy Spirit.

God is eternal. Anything united without God is temporal and will not stand.

Unity without God is quicksand — a quick way to nowhere fast!

We must make a choice to *unite* with the rock of our soul and the rock of our salvation, to walk in our God-given *Power of Unity* here on Earth as it is in Heaven.

This is how you experience *The True Power of Unity*.

Build a real one-on-one relationship and rapport with God, get to know who God is for yourself, and become one with your Creator.

- Jesus and God are one.
- Jesus is the vine.
- We are the branches.

There is no branch without the vine; therefore, without Jesus, we can do nothing.

Introduction

You must become one with your Creator.

1. One unit
2. United
3. In unity

Unity begins within you.

How can you even begin to *unite* with someone else if you can't *unite* with your True Self?

How is it that everyone is so holy, yet there is so much confusion and discord among us?

- Prayer warriors
- Full of the Holy Ghost
- Speaking in tongues
- Healing the sick
- Casting out demons

We have all this prayer, so-called faith, and spirituality, but people are suffering and not reaping the full rewards of these actions.

Most are living in lack, broken, not at God's best, and not in a place of More Than Enough.

Gossip, backbiting, tale bearing, envy, hate, jealousy, pride, selfishness, laziness, and the pure lack of basic ethics and morals reign supreme!

The Bible, which is the Word of God, is very direct, and it provides many explanations throughout both the Old and New Testament that seem to be overlooked, ignored, and/or completely misunderstood.

Satan's agenda is to steal, kill, and destroy your identity and purpose, so that you remain in darkness, outside of your rightful position, and never know who you are.

Life and abundant life are in knowing who you are, who you belong to, and what you stand for.

You must get your personal house in order. And then you will be filled with the wisdom, knowledge, and understanding that empowers you with the love that is required to maximize *The True Power of Unity!*

The True Power of Unity is within you,

Brian P. Lucas
BRIAN P. LUCAS

THE TRUE POWER OF
UNITY

Chapter 1: Unity Begins With U

The best way to implement *The True Power of Unity* is to understand the definition of *Unity*.

Unity is the state of being united or joined as a whole.

- Unity is not I, me, my, and mine.
- Unity is they, us, and we.

Unity Begins With U on the inside.

- You will not successfully unite with others until you first unite with yourself.
- You will not unite the outside until you first unite the inside.

Unity Begins With U as one unit united in unity.

1. One unit
2. United
3. In unity

You must be one unit, united with God the Father, God the Son, and God the Holy Spirit, before you will ever be able to walk in *The True Power of Unity*.

What better way to understand *The True Power of Unity* than directly from the *Source*?

Read Genesis 11:1–9

[1] And the whole earth was of <u>one</u> language, and of <u>one</u> speech.

- One Language = Unity
- One Speech = Unity

² And it came to pass, as they journeyed from the east, that they found a plain in the land of Shinar; and they dwelt there.

- They = Unity

³ And they said one to another, Go to, let us make brick, and burn them throughly. And they had brick for stone, and slime had they for morter.

- They = Unity
- Us = Unity

⁴ And they said, Go to, let us build us a city and a tower, whose top may reach unto heaven; and let us make us a name, lest we be scattered abroad upon the face of the whole earth.

- They = Unity
- Us = Unity
- We = Unity

⁵ And the LORD came down to see the city and the tower, which the children of men builded.

⁶ And the LORD said, Behold, the people is one, and they have all one language; and this they begin to do: and now nothing will be restrained from them, which they have imagined to do.

- One = Unity
- One Language = Unity
- They = Unity
- Them = Unity

⁷ Go to, let us go down, and there confound their language, that they may not understand one another's speech.

- Us = *The True Power of Unity*
- Their = Unity
- They = Unity

⁸ So the LORD scattered <u>them</u> abroad from thence upon the face of all the earth: and <u>they</u> left off to build the city.

- Them = Unity
- They = Unity

⁹ Therefore is the name of it called Babel; because the LORD did there confound the language of all the earth: and from thence did the LORD scatter them abroad upon the face of all the earth.

Read Genesis 11: 1–4

Let's highlight the words that emphasize unity in these four verses:

- (7) "They" Verses 2–4
- (5) "Us" Verses 3, 4
- (1) "We" Verse 4

Now let's review Verse 5:

⁵ And the LORD came down to see the city and the tower, which the children of men builded.

This sounds very familiar and very similar to another key ingredient and universal principle, *Faith*.

Hebrews 11:1

¹ Now Faith is the substance of things hoped for, the evidence of things not seen.

Like *Faith*, *unity* is so strong that it gets the LORD'S attention and makes Him take action.

What did the LORD do?

- Came down.

To do what?

- To see the city and the tower.

Keep in mind, this is the LORD we are talking about — the LORD who is almighty and all powerful, who created the Heavens and the Earth and everything within it.

Can the LORD not see the city and tower from Heaven?

- Of course He can.

Unity got the LORD'S attention, and the LORD came down to see the city and the tower.

So, why didn't the LORD just destroy the tower?

- Because the tower didn't have the power.

God is God, and God has all power. God could have easily just destroyed the tower, so we know that the power is not in the tower.

- The power is in the *Unity*.
- The power is in the *Faith*.

Being united as one gets the LORD'S attention and makes the LORD <u>come down</u>.

Unite with the LORD, and speak those things that are not as though they are:

- Mercy and grace *come down.*
- Anointing and favor *come down.*
- Health and wealth *come down.*
- Honor and riches *come down.*
- Prosperity and abundance *come down.*
- Truth and righteousness *come down.*
- Wisdom and knowledge *come down.*
- Faith and victory *come down.*
- More Than Enough *come down.*

One of the most important verses that provides us with a powerful example of the outcome of *unity* is verse 6:

⁶ And the LORD said, Behold, the people is one, and they have all one language; and this they begin to do: and now nothing will be restrained from them, which they have imagined to do.

Revelation:

And the LORD said, Behold the people is one [united], and they have all one [united] language; and this they begin to do [in unity]: and now NOTHING WILL BE RESTRAINED FROM THEM, WHICH THEY HAVE IMAGINED TO DO.

Why?

- Because they are united together as one.

Make It Personal:

When (Your Name) is united as one, nothing that (Your Name) has imagined to do will be restrained from (Your Name).

Division, however, is contradiction, opposition, and the *Enemy of Unity*!

Reverse the Verse:

When (Your Name) is not united as one, everything that (Your Name) has imagined to do will be restrained from (Your Name).

Most people unfortunately spend more time and energy stirring up strife and discord, which ultimately promotes and creates division, yet they wonder why they live lives that remain stagnant and unfulfilling.

How can you unite outside of yourself if you are divided within yourself? It's simple — you can't.

- Unity = *Nothing* restrained
- Division = *Everything* restrained

Matthew 12:25

²⁵ Every Kingdom divided against itself is brought to desolation; and every city or house divided against itself shall not stand.

The results of division equal desolation.

Desolation:

- Complete emptiness or destruction.
- Loneliness, sadness, unhappiness.
- Sorrow, depression, grief, and devastation.

These are the rewards you can expect to receive for division.

Think about it.

- Every Kingdom divided against itself *shall not stand.*
- Every country, state, city, or town divided against itself *shall not stand.*
- Every household, family, or church divided against itself *shall not stand.*
- Every desire, plan, or goal divided against itself *shall not stand.*

The True Power of Unity eliminates division and provides you:

- Love.
- Joy.
- Peace.
- Happiness.
- Protection.
- Fulfillment.
- Restoration.

One of the most powerful illustrations of *unity* is found in Genesis Chapter 11:1–9, yet this situation, as you can clearly see, is not positive.

Notice that in Verse 7, the LORD confounded and confused their speech:

⁷ Go to, let us go down, and there confound their language, that they may not understand one another's speech.

But why?

- Because *The True Power of Unity* is in the <u>Word</u>, and *Faith* in that <u>Word</u> comes by *hearing* that <u>Word</u>, whether it be for good or bad.

Read Romans 10:17

¹⁷ So, then Faith comes by hearing, and hearing by the word of God.

Revelation:

So, then Faith in the word of God comes by hearing the word of God.

Does a Devil worshipper have *Faith* in the Devil?

- Yes, of course they do, because *Faith* is the substance of things hoped for and the evidence of things not seen.
- So, then *Faith* in the word of Satan comes by hearing the word of Satan.

Did Adam and Eve put their Faith in the word of the serpent over the Word of God when they chose to eat the fruit of the Tree of the Knowledge of Good and Evil?

- Yes, they absolutely did, with the hopes of receiving what they heard from the serpent.
- So, then *Faith* in the word of the serpent comes by hearing the word of the serpent.

Read Genesis 11:3–4

[3] And they said one to another...

[4] And they said...

Who said?

- They said.

Before any action ever takes place:

- There is the speaking of the *Word*.
- And then the *Faith* in the *Word* spoken.

If you rightly divide the Word of Truth, you will understand that *Faith* absolutely comes by *hearing*, but that *Faith*, just like *unity*, can be for good or bad, to promote life or death.

Proverbs 18:20–21

[20] A man's belly shall be satisfied with the fruit of his mouth; and with the increase of his lips shall he be filled.

[21] Death and life are in the power of the tongue: and they that love it shall eat the fruit thereof.

Religion promotes the belief that *Unity* and *Faith* are only exercised for godliness and positivity, but this could not be further from the truth.

Proverbs 23:7

For as a person thinks in their heart so is that person:

Make It Personal:

For as [Your Name] thinks in [Your Name's] heart so is [Your Name].

Matthew 12:33–37

³³ Either make the tree good, and his fruit good; or else make the tree corrupt, and his fruit corrupt: for the tree is known by his fruit.

³⁴ O generation of vipers, how can you, being evil, speak good things? for out of the abundance of the heart the mouth speaks.

³⁵ A good man out of the good treasure of the heart bringeth forth good things: and an evil man out of the evil treasure bringeth forth evil things.

³⁶ But I say unto you, That every idle word that men shall speak, they shall give account thereof in the day of judgment.

³⁷ For by thy words thou shalt be justified, and by thy words thou shalt be condemned.

The True Power of Unity begins with the *Word*, *Faith* in the *Word*, and then acting on the *Word*.

- If the *Word* is good, then it will produce good.
- If the *Word* is evil, then it will produce evil.

This is how the *True Power of Unity* and *Faith* work for both good and evil.

This shoots a lot of necessary holes in the religious rhetoric that gets shoved down our throats nowadays.

The *True Power of Unity* cannot be obtained through religion or the foolish traditions of men. It starts with building a relationship, which is why you must study to show yourself approved.

In God, you have been provided the authority, dominion, and power.

When you have a clear understanding of *The True Power of Unity,* nothing will be withheld from you.

You will be able to boldly come before the throne of grace and call those things that are not as though they are.

Read Matthew 18:18–20

[18] Verily I say unto you, Whatsoever you shall bind on earth shall be bound in heaven: and whatsoever you shall loose on earth shall be loosed in heaven.

[19] Again I say unto you, That if two of you shall agree on earth as touching any thing that they shall ask, it shall be done for them of my Father which is in heaven.

[20] For where two or three are gathered together in my name, there am I in the midst of them.

Let's highlight the words that emphasize *unity* in these three verses:

- (5) "You" Verses 18, 19
- (1) "Two of you" Verse 19
- (1) "They" Verse 19
- (2) "Them" Verses 19, 20
- (1) "Two or three" Verse 20

Make It Personal:

Truly Jesus says unto (Your Name), Whatsoever (Your Name) shall bind on earth shall be bound in heaven: and whatsoever (Your Name) shall loose on earth shall be loosed in heaven. Again Jesus says unto (Your Name), That if two of you shall [unite and] agree on earth as touching anything that they shall ask, it shall be done for them of Jesus' Father which is in heaven. For where two or three are gathered together in Jesus' name, there is Jesus in the midst of them.

Multiple efforts focused on the same goals will reap multiple rewards, and you will truly experience the results of *The True Power of Unity*.

Look around and find a way to have more than two or three people gathered in Jesus' name, so in that moment, Jesus is in the midst.

- I need to *become one unit* with Jesus.
- I need to be *united* with Jesus.
- I need to be *in unity* with Jesus.
- I need *The True Power of Unity* in my life.

I need the power of:

- Wisdom, knowledge, understanding, discernment
- Love, joy, peace, happiness
- Grace, mercy, anointing, favor
- Prosperity, abundance, More Than Enough

I need the *Power of God* in my life:

1. One unit
2. United
3. In unity

Remember, when you are united as one, nothing will be restrained from you.

- So, what are you currently doing?
- Are you building a prideful city and tower for yourself, or are you actively engaged with others on one accord to produce *The True Power of Unity* and see God's best in your life?
- Will you allow the LORD to <u>*come down*</u> and use you in the Kingdom?
- Will you choose to *unite* to eliminate division?

Unity Begins With U:
- You are your best friend.
- You are your worst enemy.

The True Power of Unity:
1. God the Father.
2. God the Son.
3. God the Holy Spirit.

Notes:

Chapter 2: Unity Eliminates Lack

We know that *unity* is the state of being united or joined as a whole and that to truly walk in the *Power of Unity*, we must become *one unit, united, in unity* with God the Father, God the Son, and God the Holy Spirit.

To exercise the *Power of Unity* and understand how *Unity Eliminates Lack*, we must first understand the definition of lack:

- Lack is the state of being without, being in want and need due to deficiency, and not having enough of something.
- Lack is not prosperity and abundance, and it's not God's best.
- Simply put, lack is not enough.

The Bible tells us in John 10:10 that Jesus came that we may have *Life* and that we may have *Life* more abundantly.

The Bible also states in Philippians 4:13 that we can do *all things* in, by, and through Jesus Christ which strengthens us.

If Jesus has *all power* in Heaven and Earth (Matthew 28:18), Jesus came that we may have an *abundant life*, and we are able to do *all things* through Jesus, then why are there so many people — including the so-called believers — hurting and suffering in lack?

I'm suggesting to you today that the main reason is the *lack of unity*!

Genesis 11:6

⁶ And the LORD said, Behold the people is one [united], and they have all one [united] language; and this they begin to do: and now <u>NOTHING WILL BE RESTRAINED FROM THEM</u>, which they have imagined to do.

Now, let's look at this "nothing will be restrained from them."

We all know what "nothing" means, so let's review the definition for "restrained":

- To restrain is to limit, restrict, or keep under control, to prevent the freedom of movement or action, and to limit development.

So, what exactly is the Bible telling us, and what did God say?

Genesis 11:6

⁶ **<u>And the LORD said</u>**, Behold the people is one [united], and they have all one [united] language; and this they begin to do: and now <u>NOTHING WILL BE RESTRAINED FROM THEM</u>, which they have imagined to do.

Nothing will...

- Limit them.
- Restrict them.
- Keep them under control.
- Prevent their freedom of movement or action.
- Limit their development.

The LORD said that **<u>NOTHING WILL BE RESTRAINED FROM YOU</u>** when you are united as one.

I want to make sure that everyone understands that the *Power of Unity* is a universal law, just like *Faith*!

Notice, these are not godly people who the LORD said nothing would be restrained from.

- God's universal law is God's universal law.
- It's not good, and it's not bad.
- It's not right, and it's not wrong.
- It just is what it is.

It is you who decides how you are going to utilize these universal tools in your life.

You can use the *Power of Unity* and *Faith* for the Kingdom to represent the Power of God, or you have the option and the free will to choose to use it for self and the world, which ultimately contributes to the contradiction and opposition of God, making you a supporter of the *Enemy of God*.

So, if the LORD said nothing will be restrained from the ungodly, what does that say about those who choose to follow God?

Remember, Jesus has all power in Heaven and in Earth.

- Jesus is the vine.
- You are the branch.

If the vine has all power, then what does the branch have access to?

- All power!

We must become *one unit*, *united*, *in unity* with God the Father, God the Son, and God the Holy Spirit.

UNITY ELIMINATES LACK!

Psalm 23:1

[1] *The LORD is my shepherd; I shall not want.*

Make It Personal:

- I shall not *want*.
- I shall not *need*.
- I shall not *lack*.

Now, this is what God says about you, but what do you say about yourself?

You see, it's easy to read it and repeat it, but we must:

- Think it.
- Speak it.
- Believe it.
- Receive it.
- Act on what we Think, Speak, Believe, and Receive.

Luke 5:1–7

[1] And it came to pass, that, as the people pressed upon him to hear the word of God, he stood by the lake of Gennesaret,

[2] And saw two ships standing by the lake: but the fishermen were <u>gone out</u> of them, and were washing their nets.

It's hard to catch any fish when you're "gone out" of the boat. That's the problem today: Jesus is looking for us, to unite with us, but we are "gone out" and sometimes united with the wrong things.

Think about it. They have a better chance of catching fish united together on that boat rather than united to wash their nets.

[3] *And he entered into one of the ships, which was Simon's, and prayed him that he would thrust out a little from the land. And he sat down, and taught the people out of the ship.*

Jesus enters one of the ships. Jesus is showing you pictures of *unity*.

Jesus wants to enter your personal ship and is asking you to thrust out a little from the land of this world, so He can begin to teach the people out of the ship.

Note: You are the ship!

⁴ Now when he had left speaking, he said unto Simon, Launch out into the deep, and let down your nets for a draught.

Jesus said to launch out into the deep and let down your nets for a catch.

Jesus is speaking the word of direction and instruction into your life to bless you.

⁵ And Simon answering said unto him, Master, we have toiled all the night, and have taken nothing: nevertheless at thy word I will let down the net.

And what do we do? Just like Peter, we want to talk back, make excuses, explain ourselves, and be heard, rather than just uniting with Jesus and following His simple instructions to obtain our blessing.

Pay attention to these words: we have toiled all night and have taken nothing.

Here we have the word "nothing" again, but let's look at the major differences:

Genesis 11:6

The LORD said, <u>NOTHING</u> WILL BE RESTRAINED FROM THEM.

Luke 5:5–7

Here, Peter is stating that we have worked all night and have caught <u>NOTHING</u>.

- Same word.
- Same spelling.
- Totally different meaning.

The LORD is speaking of the *Power of Unity* and the results when one is united, and Peter is talking about lack, lack, and more lack!

You see, a lot of times, Jesus is giving direction and instruction and attempting to unite with us and provide for us, but instead of opening our *Eyes to See* and opening our *Ears to Hear*, we start telling Jesus about self:

- What we have done.
- What we have already tried.
- How it didn't work for us.
- Making excuses.
- Murmuring and complaining.

Many people, all over the world, sitting in their places of worship, will walk away from God the same exact way they came because they refuse to unite and become one with the true *Source* and follow the simple instructions and directions God has provided.

Finally, Peter says, at your word, Jesus, I will let down the net.

When you decide to unite with God, get with God's Program, and let down the net like Jesus said, you will begin to walk in the *Power of Unity*!

⁶ And when they had this done, they inclosed a great multitude of fishes: and their net brake.

And when they decided to unite with Jesus and did what Jesus told them to do, then the blessing came.

⁷ And they beckoned unto their partners, which were in the other ship, that they should come and help them. And they came, and filled both the ships, so that they began to sink.

And they beckoned unto their partners that they should come and help them, and they came and filled both ships.

So, what just happened here?

Once the decision was made to unite with Jesus, the blessing came — but it came in such abundance that they were forced to exercise the lesson of *unity* that they just learned from Jesus and utilize it to unite with the others, so they too could reap the rewards.

More than likely, these are the same people who were "washing their nets" together, who are now united with Jesus and receiving the blessing from the Kingdom.

Do you see how God works when you walk in the *Power of Unity?*

UNITY ELIMINATES LACK!

- I shall not *want*.
- I shall not *need*.
- I shall not *lack*.

The Bible is so amazing and so profound that mere words don't even begin to fully define its true power.

- The Bible is God's Word.
- The Bible is God speaking directly to you.

How will you obtain *The True Power of Unity* to eliminate lack if you have no basic understanding of the power, *unity,* or the Creator of both?

How can anyone even begin to attempt to become one with God if they have no idea who God is for themselves?

The Bible is your road map to obtain all the promises of God, but without the direction, navigation, guidance, and spiritual GPS system, it becomes very easy to be duped into a purposeful system of *MANipulation* and get taken advantage of by those who do not want you to obtain God's best in your life.

So, is Psalm 23:1 a reality, or is it just some line in some old story book that sits on the shelf?

Is the LORD your Shepherd, or is He not?

Did you know many people wake up every Saturday or Sunday morning and go to their place of worship with a holier-than-thou attitude and can't even afford their water or electric bill?

- Amen.
- Hallelujah.
- Praise God.
- High fives.
- Hand claps.

How can one be so holy yet live in lack?

Is this a reflection and a representation of God's best?

We must unite with *The True Power of Unity* to eliminate lack!

- I shall not *want*.
- I shall not *need*.
- I shall not *lack*.

Pay close attention right now, because this may be the eye-opener or the a-ha moment that you have been waiting for.

These next verses provide a step-by-step explanation of exactly how *The True Power of Unity* eliminates lack.

However, I'm not sure how much you are going to like it.

The Book of Acts provides us a Biblical Plan with specific requirements and a system for results.

Acts 4:31–35

³¹ And when they had prayed, the place was shaken where they were assembled together; and they were all filled with the Holy Ghost, and they spake the word of God with boldness.

- They prayed.
- They were assembled together.
- They were all filled with the Holy Ghost.
- They spoke the Word of God with boldness.

³² And the multitude of them that believed were of one heart and of one soul: neither said any of them that ought of the things which he possessed was his own; but they had all things common.

- The multitude of them that believed.
- One united heart.
- One united soul.
- They had all things common.
- No selfishness.

³³ And with great power gave the apostles witness of the resurrection of the Lord Jesus: and great grace was upon them all.

- Great grace was upon them all.

³⁴ Neither was there any among them that lacked: for as many as were possessors of lands or houses sold them, and brought the prices of the things that were sold,

- Neither was there any among them that lacked.

³⁵ And laid them down at the apostles' feet: and distribution was made unto every man according as he had need.

- Distribution was made unto every person according to their needs.

The Plan:

- Believe.
- Be of ONE (united) heart and of ONE (united) soul.
- Eliminate SELF and selfishness.
- Have ALL THINGS common.

The Requirements:

- Pray.
- Assemble together.
- ALL be filled with the Holy Ghost.
- Speak God's Word with boldness.

The System:

- Sell your belongings, and unite them together as ONE.
- Distribution is to be made to every person according to their need.

The Result:

- Great GRACE was upon them <u>ALL.</u>
- Neither was there any among them that lacked.
- No lack!
- No being without!
- No being in want and need!
- No deficiency!
- No more **NOT HAVING ENOUGH!**
- No more "I can't pay my water bill/pay my electric bill/pay my car note/put food on the table."

UNITY ELIMINATES LACK!

- I shall not *want*.
- I shall not *need*.
- I shall not *lack*.

Now, I know this may be a hard pill to swallow, but this is what the Bible says, and either the Bible is true, or the Bible is not true. It can't only be true when it fits our personal agendas.

The *Power of Unity* is a universal law, and that is why there are so many wealthy families — because whether they will admit it or not, they follow and adhere to these principles of the Bible to sustain.

Now, let me clarify one thing, so I'm not misunderstood.

I do not believe in or support socialism, and I adhere to the Wisdom of Solomon, unlike many people who feel entitled and basically want something for nothing.

A person who does not work does not eat, so freebies, handouts, getting something for nothing, and mediocrity are not the intention of this message.

If you have a lack in any area of your life, then the *Power of Unity* is missing in that area of your life. To be blunt, any place you are lacking, God is not there. I know that may be rough, but it's real.

God is a God of More Than Enough!

Remember, it's a universal law:

- When you plant apple seeds, you will get apples, not oranges.
- When you plant orange seeds, expect oranges to grow — don't expect apples.

You see, a lot of people want, but they are not willing to actually do anything to get what they want.

Many people want to be the Joseph in charge of all the land of Egypt, but they are not willing to be the Joseph who was thrown in the pit.

They want the benefits and the results of the hard work but are not willing to do the actual work.

Everyone has faith and believes until they actually need it, and then no one is anywhere to be found.

The Bible is like a photo album that provides pictures of every circumstance, situation, and scenario that we will ever face in life and presents the solutions.

Remember the bond between David and King Saul's son Jonathan?

Jonathan had a son, Mephibosheth, who detached himself from the Kingdom and was fearfully hiding in Lo-debar.

2 Samuel 9:3

³ And the king said, *Is* there not yet any of the house of Saul, that I may shew the kindness of God unto him? And Ziba said unto the king, Jonathan hath yet a son, *which is* lame on *his* feet.

King David was seeking anyone of the house of Saul to show the kindness of God. David had to seek Mephibosheth out to force *unity* and then bless him, and this is exactly what God does for us today. God seeks us out of our fears and division to unite with us and bless us out of all our lack.

God is seeking to unite with you!

Are you in position for God to show you *The True Power of Unity* and the blessings of His Kingdom?

2 Samuel 9:7

⁷ And David said unto him, Fear not: for I will surely shew thee kindness for Jonathan thy father's sake, and will restore thee all the land of Saul thy father; and thou shalt eat bread at my table continually.

Mephibosheth was living in Lo-debar in lack because of fear and the failure to unite, but once he decided to become *one unit, united, in unity,* he immediately eliminated the lack in his life.

God is telling you, fear not: He will surely show you kindness, the *Power of Unity,* and the blessings of the Kingdom when you make the decision to eliminate the lack in your life and unite with God the Father, God the Son, and God the Holy Spirit.

UNITY ELIMINATES LACK!

- I shall not *want.*
- I shall not *need.*
- I shall not *lack.*

God is a good God, and it is not His Will for you to lack or be in need. God loves you, and He has given us the greatest gift of all in Jesus. Jesus came that you may have life and have life more abundantly.

I can do all things through Christ which strengthens me.

- Jesus is the Way.
- Jesus is the Truth.
- Jesus is the Life.

Unity Eliminates Lack:

- Nothing will be restrained from you.
- Every solution to every problem is in the Word of God.

The True Power of Unity:

1. God the Father.
2. God the Son.
3. God the Holy Spirit.

Notes:

Chapter 3: The Enemy of Unity

The wolves attack and prey on the sheep. The wolves pretending to be sheep are a threat to every sheep around because they look the part, but their hearts are far away from the Truth. The wolves seek to steal, kill, and destroy every sheep in their path because that is what wolves do.

- The wolves are not sheep.
- The dogs are not cats.
- The Devil worshippers don't trust God.

This is not difficult to understand.

- The wolves will never be sheep.
- A giraffe will never be an elephant.
- A man will never be a woman.
- A woman will never be a man.

Wolves are wolves!

If the sheep were mindful of what defines a sheep, they would know that the fake sheep are wolves. The problem is the sheep are so distracted and scattered without a real shepherd that they have forgotten what the role of a sheep is. This is purposeful. Once the sheep lose focus on their own role, it allows the wolves to blend in easily without detection.

Sheep need to be sheep, and sheep need a shepherd, not a hireling. The hireling does not care for the best interests of the sheep and is therefore a proponent of the wolves.

The hireling and the wolves only care about self.

- The hireling is self-absorbed and uses the sheep for personal gain.
- The wolves pretend to be sheep to use the sheep for personal gain.

The sheep are defenseless, gullible, and naive to the plots of everyone around them, which is why they need the shepherd to lead, guide, and protect them.

- The hireling and wolves are not shepherds.
- The hireling and wolves are pretenders.

Neither one looks out for the best interests of the sheep.

The sheep are the flock, and the flock needs direction and leadership from the shepherd.

- The sheep don't lead the shepherd.
- The sheep don't protect the shepherd.
- The sheep don't provide for the shepherd.

How did we get to where we are today?

The shepherd is supposed to lead, protect, and provide for the sheep. Any sheep attempting to lead is probably a wolf in sheep's clothing. The wolves are a threat to both the sheep and the hireling because they have no problem attacking and destroying both.

Religion promotes wolves and hirelings, and neither is beneficial nor productive for the sheep. God's Word is clear, yet we continue to allow ignorance and the traditions of men to compromise and contradict it.

A sheep does not take care of, lead, provide, or protect the shepherd. The shepherd is supposed to be doing all these things for the sheep.

How far we have fallen from simple Truth!

The church now has a system and mindset that completely contradict these basic principles. It has the sheep feeling like they are responsible for the shepherd, and this is a dangerous place to be.

God is a jealous God, and the sheep are not God. It is blasphemous and extremely disrespectful to attempt to make God's sheep responsible for God's shepherd.

How does this even make sense?

It is God's responsibility to provide for His shepherd and His sheep. God never approved of the hireling or the wolves.

- The hireling will leave the sheep.
- The wolves will destroy the sheep.

This is why the sheep need a shepherd. God has ordained and sanctified those who He has appointed to tend to His flock and keep the sheep safe.

But the hireling has implemented man-made rules and regulations that incorporate the sheep taking on the role of a shepherd. This is how the wolves enter, because the sheep are taking on roles that God never permitted them to take in the first place.

- The hireling is pretending to be a shepherd.
- The wolves are pretending to be sheep.
- The sheep are confused and becoming both.

What a dangerous combination. Nobody is in their rightful position, and thus you have confusion and chaos.

- Woe unto those pretending to be shepherds but within are hirelings purposely misleading the sheep.
- Woe unto those pretending to be sheep but within are wolves purposely destroying the sheep.
- Woe unto the ignorant sheep who have decided to join the hireling and wolves.

God is real and His Word is true, and nothing shall change the Word of God. If it does not align with God's Word, do not partake in it.

Apple trees produce apples, not oranges.

- Sheep are sheep.
- Wolves are wolves.
- A hireling is a hireling.

A shepherd protects the sheep from all threats that are detrimental to the well-being of the flock.

The hireling and the wolves are really one and the same because their goals to take advantage of the sheep are aligned.

The church is full of hirelings and wolves who do not care about the well-being of God's sheep. They will continue to take everything they can under the guise of religion while the sheep remain poor, hungry, and suffering.

The shepherd provides for the sheep, but the hireling and the wolves only take from them.

This is how the hireling can live a great life of luxury while the sheep the hireling is responsible for are living in lack, malnourished.

The Enemy of Unity

How could anyone with common sense feel that this is okay?

- The so-called shepherd lives in abundance.
- The sheep live in poverty and lack.

Respectfully, this makes no sense at all. God is the Potter, and we are the clay, but God did not mold this foolishness. This is religious man-made deception at its finest.

Every sheep should have the necessities of life if they have a shepherd.

- Beware of the hireling pretending to be a shepherd.
- Beware of the wolves in sheep's clothing.
- Beware of the confused sheep who support both.

I want you to visualize in real time:

- The shepherd.
- The hireling.
- The wolves.
- The sheep.

I want this information to resonate within, so that wisdom, knowledge, and understanding can take root. I have been writing in a way to draw attention to the hireling and the wolves separately; however, you must understand that the hireling and the wolves are one and the same.

The sheep are completely out of position and have taken on the responsibility of the shepherd. The sheep feed both the hireling and the wolves. Visualize it so you can see how it makes no sense.

When was the last time you saw a sheep feed anything other than itself?

Try to visualize a sheep taking food to the shepherd, hireling, or wolves. It makes no sense at all!

This is how the so-called shepherd can live in luxury with a mansion, a private jet, and lavish vehicles, while the sheep who helped pay for it are broke, living in poverty, unable to pay their water and electric bills, and barely putting food on the table.

- How does this make sense?
- Does this sound like God's plan?

Whatever the shepherd has, the sheep should have!

Is this not what the Bible clearly declares?

How very far we have fallen from Biblical Truth!

It saddens me to see this New World Order agenda-driven church and all the foolishness attached to it that is ultimately created to keep you enslaved in religion so they continue to have control over you and your family.

Respectfully, the reason we have people in the *House of Prayer* weekly, devoted to God with the right heart, who are hurting and in need, is because those who have *Ears to Hear* God are not doing what God has instructed them to do.

I know without any doubts that God speaks to people directly and instructs them to do things to encourage, empower, and benefit others. Most people are so holy in their own minds that they do not have the *Ears to Hear* when God is speaking, and this is sad. However, some hear clearly and decide not to listen, and then people in need suffer longer unnecessarily due to the selfishness, greed, and disobedience of others.

Psalm 23:1

[1] The LORD is my shepherd; I shall not want.

The Bible clearly states that the Lord is your shepherd, and you should not want, need, or lack.

Ephesians 6:19–20

[19] And for me, that utterance may be given unto me, that I may open my mouth boldly, to make known the mystery of the gospel,

[20] For which I am an ambassador in bonds: that therein I may speak boldly, as I ought to speak.

I speak this boldly as I ought to speak before the people: No one in a *True House of Prayer* with the right heart towards God should ever be in lack or need for anything!

- Either God is God or He isn't.
- Either The Word is true or it isn't.

We must understand that the Bible is all about the King and the Kingdom.

It is not about:

- Religion.
- Rules.
- Regulations.
- Traditions.
- Denominations.
- Science.
- Democracy.
- Republic.
- Independence.
- Foolishness of men.

Again, The Bible is all about the King and the Kingdom!

Psalm 24:1

¹ The earth is the LORD'S, and the fulness thereof; the world, and they that dwell therein.

The King owns everything and everyone!

When you truly understand that all you have and possess belongs to God, it makes it so much easier to be obedient to His voice when it comes time to distribute to others. Only a person who thinks that what they have belongs to them will struggle in this area.

You must understand that you do not own anything!

One of the biggest tricks and deceptions of the World's System is making you think that you own something.

Everything, including yourself, belongs to God!

Everything you have, all that you possess, belongs to God and has been placed under your management to help someone else. Every gift and talent God has ordained and sanctified you with is for someone else, not yourself.

When we truly understand this, it is very difficult to fall into pride, arrogance, greed, envy, selfishness, and so many other traps of the World's System that keep us from the Truth.

You need to know that you own nothing!

This will make it easier to obey the Owner when He speaks and tells you what to do with what He has blessed you with to fulfill a specific purpose, because you understand it all belongs to Him.

Psalm 55:22

²² Cast thy burden upon the LORD, and he shall sustain thee: he shall never suffer the righteous to be moved.

When you know who you are, who you belong to, and what you stand for, the Truth will become clear to you, and you will truly understand casting your cares upon Him.

The sheep need the shepherd, and the shepherd needs the sheep, or else he is not a shepherd.

The sheep are nothing without the Shepherd!

- You are nothing without God.
- You have nothing without Jesus.
- You have no power without the Holy Spirit.

The hirelings and wolves of religion are distractions that cause confusion to compromise and contradict God's Word, just like the serpent in the garden with Adam and Eve.

- Open your *Eyes to See* the Light over darkness.
- Open your *Ears to Hear* the Truth over the lie.

Satan is crafty, and he only comes to steal, kill, and destroy your identity to keep you from knowing who you truly are.

Satan must destroy *unity* and cause division, and this is the true role of the hireling and the wolves. They are assigned by Satan to scatter the sheep away from the *True Shepherd* so that they are easily destroyed.

John 10:10–16

[10] The thief comes not, but for to steal, and to kill, and to destroy: I [Jesus] am come that [the people] might have life, and that [the people] might have [life] more abundantly.

[11] I [Jesus] am the good shepherd: the good shepherd giveth his life for the sheep.

¹² But [the person] that is a hireling, and is not the shepherd, who does not own the sheep, sees the wolf coming, and leaves the sheep, and flees: and the wolf catches [the sheep], and scatters the sheep.

¹³ The hireling flees, because he is a hireling, and cares not for the sheep.

¹⁴ I [Jesus] am the good shepherd, and [I Jesus] know my sheep, and am known of mine.

¹⁵ As the Father [God] knows [Jesus], even so I [Jesus] know the Father [God]: and I [Jesus] lay down my life for the sheep.

¹⁶ And other sheep I [Jesus] have, which are not of this fold: [those other sheep] I must also bring, and [those other sheep] shall hear [Jesus'] voice; and there shall be one fold, and one shepherd.

- Jesus is the *Good Shepherd*.
- Jesus gave His life for us.
- In Jesus we are united as one-fold with one shepherd.

The Enemy of Unity:

- Division from the Truth.
- Compromise of the Truth.
- Contradiction of the Truth.
- Distraction from the Truth.

All of these are clear reflections and representations of Satan, who is the father of lies, and the tool he uses, which is religion. *The Enemy of Unity* is Satan himself and religion.

The True Power of Unity:

1. God the Father
2. God the Son
3. God the Holy Spirit

Chapter 4: Beware of Prideful Unity

A very simple definition of "prideful" is:
- Thinking too highly of oneself.
- Conceited.
- Arrogant.
- Overconfident.

Anything and everything we do that we place before God in any shape, form, or fashion is prideful.

The best example we have of pride begins with Satan, who thinks too highly of himself and becomes conceited, arrogant, and overconfident and attempts to replace God.

This is foolish because the created will never be able to outweigh or outperform the Creator of all things.

We must be careful not to allow *The True Power of Unity* to fall into this unhealthy area of pride.

Satan gives us a great example of what not to do, which we can read in Isaiah, Ezekiel, and the Book of Revelation.

Isaiah 14:12–23

[12] How art thou fallen from heaven, O Lucifer, son of the morning! how art thou cut down to the ground, which didst weaken the nations!

- Pride weakens the nations.
- Pride comes before the fall.
- Pride will get you cut down.

¹³ For thou hast said in thine heart, I will ascend into heaven, I will exalt my throne above the stars of God: I will sit also upon the mount of the congregation, in the sides of the north:

- Pride ascends self above Heaven.
- Pride exalts self above the stars of God.
- Pride promotes self.

¹⁴ I will ascend above the heights of the clouds; I will be like the most High.

- Pride ascends self above the clouds.
- Pride provides a false sense of entitlement.

¹⁵ Yet thou shalt be brought down to hell, to the sides of the pit.

- Pride that positions self above Truth will bring you down.

¹⁶ They that see thee shall narrowly look upon thee, and consider thee, saying, Is this the man that made the earth to tremble, that did shake kingdoms;

- Pride that boasts self will be examined by others.

¹⁷ That made the world as a wilderness, and destroyed the cities thereof; that opened not the house of his prisoners?

- Pride will be exposed by Truth.

¹⁸ All the kings of the nations, even all of them, lie in glory, every one in his own house.

¹⁹ But thou art cast out of thy grave like an abominable branch, and as the raiment of those that are slain, thrust through with a sword, that go down to the stones of the pit; as a carcase trodden under feet.

- Pride will cast you out.
- Pride is abominable.
- Pride will eventually be destroyed.

²⁰ Thou shalt not be joined with them in burial, because thou hast destroyed thy land, and slain thy people: the seed of evildoers shall never be renowned.

- Pride will not be united with Truth.
- Pride shall never be renowned.

²¹ Prepare slaughter for his children for the iniquity of their fathers; that they do not rise, nor possess the land, nor fill the face of the world with cities.

- Pride destroys you and your family.
- Pride eliminates the rise, possession, and fulfillment.

²² For I will rise up against them, saith the LORD of hosts, and cut off from Babylon the name, and remnant, and son, and nephew, saith the LORD.

- The LORD will rise up against every form of Prideful Unity.

²³ I will also make it a possession for the bittern, and pools of water: and I will sweep it with the besom of destruction, saith the LORD of hosts.

- The LORD will completely destroy every form of *Prideful Unity*.

Ezekiel 28:11–19

¹¹ Moreover the word of the LORD came unto me, saying,

¹² Son of man, take up a lamentation upon the king of Tyrus, and say unto him, Thus saith the Lord GOD; Thou sealest up the sum, full of wisdom, and perfect in beauty.

¹³ Thou hast been in Eden the garden of God; every precious stone was thy covering, the sardius, topaz, and the diamond, the beryl, the onyx, and the jasper, the sapphire, the emerald, and the carbuncle, and gold: the workmanship of thy tabrets and of thy pipes was prepared in thee in the day that thou wast created.

¹⁴ Thou art the anointed cherub that covereth; and I have set thee so: thou wast upon the holy mountain of God; thou hast walked up and down in the midst of the stones of fire.

¹⁵ Thou wast perfect in thy ways from the day that thou wast created, till iniquity was found in thee.

¹⁶ By the multitude of thy merchandise they have filled the midst of thee with violence, and thou hast sinned: therefore I will cast thee as profane out of the mountain of God: and I will destroy thee, O covering cherub, from the midst of the stones of fire.

¹⁷ Thine heart was lifted up because of thy beauty, thou hast corrupted thy wisdom by reason of thy brightness: I will cast thee to the ground, I will lay thee before kings, that they may behold thee.

¹⁸ Thou hast defiled thy sanctuaries by the multitude of thine iniquities, by the iniquity of thy traffick; therefore will I bring forth a fire from the midst of thee, it shall devour thee, and I will bring thee to ashes upon the earth in the sight of all them that behold thee.

¹⁹ All they that know thee among the people shall be astonished at thee: thou shalt be a terror, and never shalt thou be any more.

God illustrates the power, wisdom, and beauty of His creation in full detail so we clearly understand that there is nothing wrong with what God has created.

Beware of Prideful Unity

Like the anointed cherub, we have all been fearfully and wonderfully made by the hand of God, with gifts and talents to fulfill His purpose. What God created is never the issue; it is what we do with what God has blessed us with that brings about the pride that He detests.

The Bible states that what He created was full of wisdom, beauty, and perfection until the day iniquity was found in him and he sinned against God.

When we become prideful within, we are uniting ourselves with the opposition and going against God.

Prideful Unity will only lead to destruction in the end.

Revelations 12:7–12

⁷ And there was war in heaven: Michael and his angels fought against the dragon; and the dragon fought and his angels.

- The dragon is full of pride.
- The dragon unites with his angels to go against God.
- *Prideful Unity* against God causes war.

⁸ And prevailed not; neither was their place found any more in heaven.

- *Prideful Unity* against God will not prevail.

⁹ And the great dragon was cast out, that old serpent, called the Devil, and Satan, which deceiveth the whole world: he was cast out into the earth, and his angels were cast out with him.

- *Prideful Unity* deceives the whole world.
- *Prideful Unity* is cast out of God's presence.

¹⁰ And I heard a loud voice saying in heaven, Now is come salvation, and strength, and the kingdom of our God, and the power of his Christ: for the accuser of our brethren is cast down, which accused them before our God day and night.

- Salvation, strength, kingdom, and the power are within *The True Power of Unity*.
- *Prideful Unity* is the opposition that is cast down.

¹¹ And they overcame him by the blood of the Lamb, and by the word of their testimony; and they loved not their lives unto the death.

- *The True Power of Unity* overcomes *Prideful Unity*.

¹² Therefore rejoice, ye heavens, and ye that dwell in them. Woe to the inhabiters of the earth and of the sea! for the devil is come down unto you, having great wrath, because he knoweth that he hath but a short time.

- *Prideful Unity* has come down unto us from the Devil to destroy our identity and our relationship with our Creator God the Father.

Pride in self ultimately eliminates God and encourages and empowers us to place ourselves before Him. This is the closest to the Devil that one can ever be. If you are not for God, then you are against God, and if you are against God, then you are supporting the Devil.

Pride places self before God and is equivalent to worshipping self over God, which is the same as worshipping the Devil in the form of *Prideful Unity*.

We can see this taking place with Adam and Eve in the garden in the Book of Genesis and with the chief priests and Pharisees in the Gospel of John.

Beware of Prideful Unity

Genesis 3:1–15

¹ Now the serpent was more subtil than any beast of the field which the LORD God had made. And he said unto the woman, Yea, hath God said, Ye shall not eat of every tree of the garden?

- The serpent uses craftiness to engage in conversation with Eve.

² And the woman said unto the serpent, We may eat of the fruit of the trees of the garden:

- Eve responds in *unity* with what she knows to be the Truth.

³ But of the fruit of the tree which is in the midst of the garden, God hath said, Ye shall not eat of it, neither shall ye touch it, lest ye die.

- Eve's faith displays *unity* in what she knows to be the Truth.

⁴ And the serpent said unto the woman, Ye shall not surely die:

- The serpent provides opposition and an option to unite with his word over God's Word.

⁵ For God doth know that in the day ye eat thereof, then your eyes shall be opened, and ye shall be as gods, knowing good and evil.

- The serpent provides Eve with the option to indulge in *Prideful Unity* outside of God.

⁶ And when the woman saw that the tree was good for food, and that it was pleasant to the eyes, and a tree to be desired to make one wise, she took of the fruit thereof, and did eat, and gave also unto her husband with her; and he did eat.

- Pride focuses on self rather than God's Word.
- Pride sees self-will over God's Will.

- Pride desires the opposition of God's Word.
- Pride has an appetite for self-indulgence.
- *Prideful Unity* empowers others to join in.

⁷ And the eyes of them both were opened, and they knew that they were naked; and they sewed fig leaves together, and made themselves aprons.

- *Prideful Unity* empowers the natural man.

⁸ And they heard the voice of the LORD God walking in the garden in the cool of the day: and Adam and his wife hid themselves from the presence of the LORD God amongst the trees of the garden.

- *Prideful Unity* attempts to hide from the LORD.

⁹ And the LORD God called unto Adam, and said unto him, Where art thou?

- *Prideful Unity* destroys your connection with God.

¹⁰ And he said, I heard thy voice in the garden, and I was afraid, because I was naked; and I hid myself.

- *Prideful Unity* empowers and encourages fear, which is a spirit that does not come from God.

¹¹ And he said, Who told thee that thou wast naked? Hast thou eaten of the tree, whereof I commanded thee that thou shouldest not eat?

- *Prideful Unity* enabled them to put their faith in the word of the serpent instead of the Word of God.

¹² And the man said, The woman whom thou gavest to be with me, she gave me of the tree, and I did eat.

- *Prideful Unity* creates a blame-shifting mentality and mindset that refuses to take responsibility.

¹³ And the LORD God said unto the woman, What is this that thou hast done? And the woman said, The serpent beguiled me, and I did eat.

- *Prideful Unity* encourages others to blame-shift and refuse to take responsibility.

¹⁴ And the LORD God said unto the serpent, Because thou hast done this, thou art cursed above all cattle, and above every beast of the field; upon thy belly shalt thou go, and dust shalt thou eat all the days of thy life:

- *Prideful Unity* is cursed by God and will not sustain.

¹⁵ And I will put enmity between thee and the woman, and between thy seed and her seed; it shall bruise thy head, and thou shalt bruise his heel.

- *Prideful Unity* ultimately causes division.
- *The True Power of Unity* will destroy *Prideful Unity*.

We must understand that Satan has already lost the war regardless of what happens in the natural battles that take place here in the Earth realm. The spiritual always goes before the natural, God's Word will never return to Him void, and what He has spoken is already finished.

Genesis 3:15 explains clearly from the beginning that Jesus will crush Satan's head. This is exactly what happened when Jesus sacrificed His life for us as the Lamb of God.

Like Satan and the serpent, the religious leaders formed a *Prideful Unity* to destroy and ultimately kill Jesus.

John 11:47–48

⁴⁷ Then gathered the chief priests and the Pharisees a council, and said, What do we? for this man doeth many miracles.

- *Prideful Unity* plots to stop the gift of God.

⁴⁸ If we let him thus alone, all men will believe on him: and the Romans shall come and take away both our place and nation.

- *Prideful Unity* attacks innocence.
- *Prideful Unity* attacks Truth.
- *Prideful Unity* attacks Faith in Truth.
- *Prideful Unity* is more concerned about titles and positions than Truth.

John 12:19

¹⁹ The Pharisees therefore said among themselves, Perceive ye how ye prevail nothing? behold, the world is gone after him.

- *Prideful Unity* will not prevail.

We must understand the importance of *Prideful Unity* because it is detrimental to our success and well-being.

Prideful Unity will take the very people who are supposed to be the reflection and representation of *The True Power of Unity* and allow them to be used by Satan to destroy the Truth.

We must realize that this way of thinking is amongst us today and that there is nothing new under the sun.

Many people who are so-called leaders and followers of the Truth are nothing more than walking, talking lies, who worship the father of lies.

When you step out of *The True Power of Unity*, you step into fear, which is the enemy of your Faith in God's Word.

What happened when Adam and Eve decided to unite together against God?

They became:

- Naked.
- Alone.
- Without.

They were:

- Missing something.
- Wanting something.
- Needing something.
- In lack, not having enough.

So, where art thou?

Are you walking in *The True Power of Unity* with God, or is God still looking for you because you are <u>naked</u> and <u>afraid</u>?

Without God and *The True Power of Unity* in your life, there is lack in your life!

Our God is a Good God!

Beware of Prideful Unity:

- I shall not fear.
- I shall not be afraid.
- I shall not hide.

The True Power of Unity:

1. God the Father
2. God the Son
3. God the Holy Spirit

Notes:

Chapter 5: Destructive Unity

Some of the most talented people are also the most broken and most easily destroyed by brainwashing and conditioning. The system of the world minimizes greatness for you, so that your gift is ultimately controlled to promote the world.

You are at your greatest with your God-given talents alone. The system of the world *MANipulates* you into using what was placed inside of you to honor God for yourself, and then it slowly but surely enslaves you into a system where you do not belong.

Then we all wonder how this great talent that was once used to honor God became so tainted and distorted. The system of this world is a destroyer of all that is good, and it presents you with alternative options that are detrimental to your elevation, growth, and development.

The World's System pretends to have your best interests in mind, but their intentions will always line up with the promotion of death and the agenda of depopulation.

I write way too many truths than most are comfortable with, so they make every excuse to stay as far away as possible until they want or need something, and then they show their fictitious faces to get what they desire from me.

People are very selfish and extremely hypocritical, if you really pay attention to their motives. The World's System has tricked them into thinking that this is just the way the world works, so it is best to get on board with lies rather than be left behind or be unaccepted by the masses.

Most people have this lazy "get in where I fit in" mentality. There is no true benefit in putting the real you in timeout just to appease the crooked people of this world that we live in. Stay true to who you are and stand up to that truth until the day you die. Do not be hustled and conned by this deceitful system that only wants to control and enslave you for its personal gain and benefit. Do not be so naive and gullible when it comes to your truth.

The World's System does not care about you or your family. They only want to take what they can while they can, until there is nothing left of yourself to offer. This is their agenda from the beginning. Satan has empowered them to steal, kill, and destroy the identity of you and your family and to keep you from fulfilling your God-given assignment.

I could easily share this same information and keep God, Jesus, and the Spirit out of it. It would be more accepted and appreciated in this World's System, but this system is not my system. I am in this world, but I am not of this world.

People with talent are so quick to take the God out of the gift that God gave them to appease to the system of the world. This is the true definition of selling yourself out to benefit the *Enemy and the Opposition.*

I refuse to comply with the offers of man that discredit, disrespect, and ultimately contradict the Word of God. No amount of money or fame is worth the end result because Hell does not care about any of these things. Your money, fame, title, and worldly accomplishments mean absolutely nothing when death is knocking at your door.

- You can't buy God.
- You can't buy Salvation.
- You can't buy Truth.
- You can't buy True Freedom.

Your accomplishments in the World's System have no authority, dominion, or power in the Kingdom of Heaven or the Kingdom of God. God is neither impressed nor moved by watching the gift you received from Him being utilized to fulfill the lusts of the flesh. You will give an account for every time you failed to fulfill the assignment that your gift was created for.

Respectfully, this is raw truth without judgment. Judging is not my place nor my calling. God has ordained and sanctified me to deliver a word to empower you that most people are not bold enough to speak. Lying and being fake is so much easier and more accepted and appreciated than the Truth.

Why is that? Because looking in the mirror that exposes you is not always the best feeling. Honesty tends to hurt people. When lies are the new status quo, we allow the system of the world to destroy us every day we do not speak against it.

We are all one and the same, and no one is better or worse than the other. However, when you do not know who you are, you may feel the pull to side with the ways of the World's System, even when you know deep down that something about it does not feel right.

We must be strong enough to listen to that small voice inside that exposes the fakeness around us and highlights the lies that the World's System continues to shove down our throats. Deep down, we know that something about this New World Order movement is wrong, yet we still side with it and encourage it.

Why are we supporting what we already know is not the Truth?

I watch the very few who are in positions to reach the masses pouring out their hearts, trying to get you to finally see and accept Truth. But they are ridiculed, mocked, written off as crazy, and despised by the powers that be, simply for trying to help you know the Truth.

I am not foolish enough to go into more depth here and name any names because I am not led by the Spirit to do so.

Keep in mind that the people the Devil has put in place to attack you and your family are the same people providing you with what you see and hear every day by way of entertainment in every form and fashion.

Satan is crafty — he knows what he is doing. Many things we ignore and write off are the very things that hold Truth.

We have all heard the claims about fake news recently, and this is nothing new. Any news or information that is provided to you that is not Truth is indeed fake. So, yes fake news is absolutely a real thing.

Fake News	Fake People	Fake Choice
Fake Reality	Fake Education	Fake Opinion
Fake History	Fake Power	Fake Assistance
Fake Opportunity	Fake Leadership	Fake Disagreement

All of these apply and are highly active and promoted in the World's System daily to keep you as far away from the Truth as possible.

If you can just listen past the rhetoric and have *Ears to Hear* past the joke that is being told, to digest the actual words being spoken and not just the beat being played...

If you have the *Eyes to See* the hidden messages rather than just being entertained by the movie, series, or cartoon you are watching...

Then and only then will the secrets that the system of the world does not want you to know be revealed to you and your family.

It amazes me how all the "crazy conspiracy theory people on drugs who are completely out of control" always end up the same way.

- Silenced/blackballed/incarcerated.
- Plane/helicopter/vehicle accident.
- Slip and fall or drowning accident.
- Suicide/drug overdose.
- Accused of child/sex abuse.

I have the utmost respect for those who were attacked but remained true to the Truth instead of having the typical "If I can't beat them, then I may as well join them" attitude.

Those who make the decision to join the lie do it knowing full well that they will be destroying and manipulating their own people, yet they proceed for selfish gain. This is the lowest of the low.

It is no secret to those of us who are awake and aware. We know exactly what these people sacrifice to obtain these temporary worldly positions. They try their best to hide behind the body art and these fictitious characters they have created. But those of us with *Eyes to See* know that this is nothing more than a facade to cover up their filthy, disgusting shame for doing what they had to do to be in the inner circle.

These people have taken the talents and gifts that God gave them to build up others for the Kingdom of God and have decided to use them as tools to promote the World's System and destroy God's people in the process, and then they have the audacity to get up on a stage and pretend to thank the God of the Bible for this betrayal. The only god they are thanking is the god of this world, which is none other than Satan, Lucifer, and the Devil, who is empowering them to use their God-given gifts for the things of this world.

Do not be tricked by the trap of all traps. Every person who knowingly preys on God's people will be held accountable, whether it be in this life or after.

- We cannot hustle God.
- We cannot pimp God.
- We cannot outsmart God.

God is God, and He is above all.

Destructive Unity:

- God's gifts and talents used for self.
- God's gifts and talents used for Satan.
- God's gifts and talents used to destroy God's people.

The True Power of Unity:

1. God the Father
2. God the Son
3. God the Holy Spirit

Appendix: Divide to Conquer

What God has placed in you cannot be duplicated or denied. God has equipped you to fulfill His purpose amongst the *Enemy and Opposition*, which is why your gift will put you before great people.

The Spirit of God will make Himself known and speak directly through you to encourage and empower others to realize that it is God that they are missing.

The void and emptiness on the inside of a person is the true meaning of "lost." For a person to be lost, they must have at one point been there. You cannot be lost from a place or position if you were never there.

The original intent and rightful position were stripped away from you because of Adam and Eve's choice to put their faith in the contradiction of God's Word. This allowed the knowledge of good and evil to enter, which ultimately invited, encouraged, and empowered sin. This sin, which is death and the separation from life, is the reason we are all born into this world lost.

We are in this world, but we are not of this world. This is not God's original intent. We are born out of position in a system that is not godly.

There is no life in the World's System. There is only death and the motives and ambitions to promote more death.

Until you find the way to the Truth, there is no life. We are all born the walking dead, far from where we originally were. Our mission in life is to get back to our rightful position.

The Kingdom mentality and mindset must be reborn to transition you back to the right system. There must be a renewal of the mind and a rebirth to reprogram you to be the person God created you to be.

You have been tainted, brainwashed, and conditioned to partake in the World's System, which has enslaved you with the foolishness, doctrines, religions, and traditions of men.

Man is not your God, and man is not your teacher!

You will not find your truth in the hands of man. Satan has manipulated man to utilize the Word of God and the power of the Bible to enslave you with rules, regulations, traditions, and the foolishness of man.

Instead of empowering you with the Truth, they take bits and pieces of the Truth to form a great lie to keep you blind and confused for their own selfish gain.

God empowers *unity* and in all things is the perfect example of *unity*.

- God the Father
- Jesus Christ the Son of God
- The Holy Spirit of God

All one and the same and united as one.

But what does man do? Where is *unity*?

Man, by the tricks and deception of Satan, causes division in everything they touch and try to do outside of Truth.

I want you to really think about what I am telling you right now. This is extremely important information.

Appendix: Divide to Conquer

In war, there is the understanding that you must *Divide to Conquer*, which is basically division.

The Bible declares that with *unity*, nothing will be withheld from you. So, why does man spend all their time focused on providing the complete opposite?

You cannot successfully control or enslave a united group unless you provide a fictitious reality of *unity* to the united group.

The goal is always to control you and keep you where they want you to be, so you are never a threat to their agenda. They pretend to be for you and your family's best interests and pretend to give you a choice when you never really have a say in the matter in the first place.

I won't go too deep into this subject in this book, but politics is a great example of what I am referring to here.

Democrats and Republicans are like the Twix commercials.

- Pick a side
- Left or right

But the way you hold the package will determine whether the side you pick is truly left or truly right, and that may change daily, unbeknownst to you. Like the Twix commercials, politics provides you with a fictitious choice. It is a masterful illusion.

Everything man does attempting to be God causes unnecessary division, which is all a part of the plan. They must divide us to conquer us to remain in a position of control over us. They must *Divide to Conquer*.

Look at religion:

- Catholics
- Christians
- Muslims
- Buddhists
- Hindus
- And many more

1. Are any of these religions truly united?

Look at the denominations:

- Pentecostal
- Baptist
- Methodist
- Holiness
- 7th Day Adventists
- Mormons
- Latter-day Saints
- Lutheran
- Presbyterian
- Jehovah's Witnesses
- Even non-denominational

2. Are any of these denominations truly united?

Look at the government:

- President
- Vice President
- Senators
- Congressmen
- Governors
- Mayors

- Judges
- State Officials

3. Are any of these government entities truly united?

Look at the military:

- Air Force
- Army
- Coast Guard
- Marines
- Navy
- Space Force

4. Are any of these military forces truly united?

Look at the cultural groups:

- Black Israelites
- Black Lives Matter
- Black Panther
- KKK
- NAACP
- White Supremacist Groups
- And many more

5. Are any of these so-called groups truly united?

Look at street gangs:

- Bloods
- Crips
- Gangsters
- Vice Lords
- And many more

6. Are any of these gangs truly united?

Now, let's look at the humans:

- Black
- Brown
- Red
- White
- Yellow

7. Are any of us truly united?

No, absolutely not!

Every one of the groups listed gives the illusion of *unity* within, but they are not united as a whole or within.

They are all divided!

1. Catholics and Christians are religions, but do they believe the same things?
2. Pentecostal and Baptist are denominations, but do they agree?
3. Governors and Mayors are both part of the government structure, but are they on the same page?
4. The Air Force and the Army are both branches of the military, but do they have respect for each other?
5. Bloods and Crips are both gangs, but do they believe the same things?
6. Black Panthers and the White Supremacists are both cultural groups, but do they see eye to eye?
7. Humanity is the only race that exists. Are we united?

No, we are not united. These groups do not get along with each other, nor do they get along within themselves. There is division at every turn, outside and within, and this is purposeful.

Division is the design from the beginning!

They need you to want to be a part of something that empowers a sense of *unity* but simultaneously strips you of the very *unity* you desire.

If these fake options work so well:

- Why does it feel like the world is falling apart?
- Why is there so much chaos and confusion?
- Why does no one seem to get along?
- Why is there so much hurt, pain, and suffering?

The answer is Division! To Divide you is to Conquer you!

This is not God's original plan for you and your family.

Divide to Conquer:

- Provide a fictitious choice.
- Promote division under the guise of unity.

The True Power of Unity:

1. God the Father
2. God the Son
3. God the Holy Spirit

Notes:

Bonus Chapter: Purpose to Impact

It may be offensive, but remember, the message that comes from the man of God starts with the man of God. This means that God gives the person the message, and it's for that person first, and then that person is responsible to go and convey what God has taught them and give it to you.

So, anything that is offensive is only offensive because it resonates. If you're offended, it's because a mirror is in your face.

Don't be mad at the vessel because it is only God speaking through me. I'm only going to say what I have been led to say, but I had to deal with it myself first. So, remember, anything I say that may offend you, I offended myself with first.

I know that when we first hear a message, sometimes we hear it in the natural, but we are dealing with spiritual warfare.

I understand that this message is not for everybody. There are people reading this right now who will not get it. It just is what it is. They will probably get it five years from now, but will it be too late?

The church is walking blindly because their vision has become clouded by the things of the world that do not align with God's will. The shepherds have set their sights on success, money, fame, and power, which have become their gods. Rather than doing God's will and allowing God to provide, they have chosen to use God's name as a platform to forge their own wealth on the back of God's people.

They have given in to compromise and developed church traditions for personal, selfish gain, allowing the enemy to walk in through the front door, sit on the front row, and conjure up distractions and wreak havoc in the house of God. Thus, the sheep are lost. Many lack wisdom and knowledge and continue to live in spiritual bondage.

God is raising up a radical army with unconventional *Eyes to See* and perfectly tuned *Ears to Hear* His voice. They, the radical army, will possess special gifts to escape the maze of deceit that the leaders who walked before them fell victim to. They will be a light in the world full of darkness to lead God's people in these final days.

We've got to stop playing church.

- When are we going to wake up?
- When are we going to rise to the occasion?

Jesus is the rock of my soul and the rock of my salvation.

Why does it seem like everybody is standing in the sand?

The church is supposed to be a place of healing, but it has become an entertainment factory following the ways of the world.

The church is supposed to lead the world. The world is supposed to follow the church. But what do we do? Have service and turn the lights off, swing lights around, and do exactly what you see at a concert.

We have become the epitome of what we are supposed to be against. Think about it. The way of the world is shifting and leaving the church behind, when the church is supposed to come before the world and lead it.

Remember back in the day when something crazy would happen, the preachers would get together, and about a week later, maybe two or three days, the issue was solved?

They want to put silly stuff on boxes. We'll go and have a revolution and stir up something, and that box will come off the shelf.

- They want to talk about things we don't want to hear about.
- They put things on TV that are not right.
- They play music that sounds like garbage.

The people get together, and they have prayer, not marching and poster boards. The church got together and prayed, and the church did something, and then whatever the issue was seemed to disappear.

Where is the church now?

We've got alphabet soup, taste the rainbow, and your kids are being taught all manner of things that you don't really even know about because you don't pay attention.

This is what is happening in the world. I don't even have kids, and I know. So, what's the excuse?

The church is supposed to be the leading and dominating factor in the world. And when I say the church, I don't mean a building. Not the smallest building or the grandest one.

I am referring to the inside of your heart. Your heart must be right. What's in you is what's going to make a difference in the world. That is what is going to lead, guide, and direct this nation into a different situation, but it's not going to happen with people sitting around doing nothing.

That's why I love the name of this chapter and specifically the word "impact."

Impact: To have a strong effect on someone or something.

- Does salvation have a strong effect?
- Does healing have a strong effect?

Pick whatever word you want that has a positive impact. That's what the church is supposed to be for.

We've got to wake up and rise and take a stand.

- Those who know that God is God.
- Those who know who they are.
- Those who know who they belong to.
- Those who know what God has done for them and their purpose.

We must take a stand. We can no longer go to church, sit in chairs, and high-five our neighbors. No disrespect to that, but it's got to be more than high-fiving your neighbor. Do you know what I'm saying? There has to be more than that. I can't just high-five my neighbor and expect things to change in the world. It's not going to happen.

- I can't high-five my neighbor.
- I can't do mime dances.
- I can't do twirls.
- I can't fling flags around.
- I can't flash lights.

That's silliness, if there isn't any perspective behind it. Now if I'm high-fiving you and there is spirit behind it and there is something that we are doing, and there is a connection, alright then.

But what is the benefit if we just high-five each other, and then we go home still broke, sick, with unforgiveness, feeling the same way we felt before we came?

This isn't a book of entertainment, and I'm not writing to entertain you.

People may think because it's coming this rough that it can't be God. Oh, it's God.

It's God because I don't do this. One thing about somebody who is preaching, and anybody will tell you, is that they don't want to preach. I don't want to preach or write these messages.

- I'm writing because I have to write.
- I'm writing because I'm ordained to write.
- I'm writing because that is what I am called to do.

Any time I try to run away from it, I end up with a mic or a pen in my hand again. Because people see some things in you more than what you see in yourself.

Most of the time, when you think you know the Bible and you think you've got the *Eyes to See*, it's actually the people around you who have the *Eyes to See*.

You aren't looking in that mirror I was just talking about, so sometimes it takes the people around you to push you in the right direction.

Alright, let's get to this message.

We're going to read from Jeremiah 1:4–5 and Ecclesiastes 3:1.

Jeremiah 1:4–5

[4] Then the word of the Lord came unto Jeremiah, saying,

⁵ Before I (God) formed you in the belly (Jeremiah) I knew you; and before you came forth out of the womb (Jeremiah) I sanctified you, and (Jeremiah) I ordained you a prophet unto the nations.

Ecclesiastes 3:1

¹ To everything there is a season, and a time to every purpose under heaven.

The title of this message is:

Purpose to Impact

"Season and Time"

Here are the questions we usually ask ourselves.

- Why am I here?
- What is my purpose?
- What is my reason for living?

The answer is very, very simple: to impact the lives of God's people. God has given you *Purpose to Impact* the lives of His people.

I can spend practically until Jesus comes back on the first part of Verse 5 in Jeremiah.

- Before I formed you.
- Before I formed you in the belly.

God is the "I AM." I AM THAT I AM.

You were before you were. I'm trying to tell you about the calling you have now. I'm trying to tell you about what's in you, what's real about you.

Before you were formed, you were.

It's hard to understand, but before Jesus was here, He was here. You know that, right?

Before I formed you in the belly, I knew you.

And before you came into the world, before you were born, what did He do?

- He sanctified you.

So, before I even came out crying and whining, God knew me, and God sanctified me before I was ever here.

We're not done there.

And I ordained you, for Jeremiah now, a prophet unto the nations.

So, since God is no respecter of persons and is the same yesterday, today, and forever, if Jeremiah was known before Jeremiah was born and before he was formed, what does that say about you?

This verse applies to everybody. This is Jeremiah writing down what happened for Jeremiah, but we know God is not a respecter of persons.

- Before you were formed in the belly.
- Before you were born, you were sanctified.
- Before you were born, you were ordained to be something and someone among the nations.

We are here to talk about *Purpose to Impact: Season and Time* because you are supposed to be here for something.

- You are not supposed to be here taking up space.
- You are not supposed to be here just breathing God's air, feeling all free.
- You are not supposed to be like the leaves that blow whichever way the wind blows.

You're supposed to have a standard. You're supposed to be what God has ordained you to be. That's why when you try to go do what you want to do, it never works. And when it does seem to work, the Devil takes it all back because sometimes you have bad success. The Bible talks about good success, which means there is an opposite... bad success.

Before you were formed, God already knew you. Because God is Spirit, and those who worship God must worship God in spirit and in truth. And the Bible tells you in Genesis that you were made after God's image and God's likeness.

So how was I formed before I was?

- Because you are not what you see when you look in the mirror.
- You were here before you were here.

This is going to go over so many heads.

Before you were, you were. Before you became what you see when you look in the mirror, you were already here.

That's going to blow too many of you away. You were here already.

You are a spirit, a speaking spirit that has the power, authority, and dominion that was given in Genesis and taken away when they ate the fruit.

What do you think Jesus came back for?

- To high-five with you?
- To do cartwheels?
- To entertain you?

Jesus came back to take back the power that we gave away. So, you are a speaking spirit with authority, dominion, and power, who was known by God before you were formed and sanctified before you came out of the belly.

And you are ordained to do _____.

You must fill in the blank yourself because only you will know the answer.

I know what I'm supposed to do. It took me 40 years, but I know. Actually, I knew all along; I just didn't want to do it.

There is something on the inside of you that has been placed there to make a difference in this ridiculous place we call the world, which is so Satanic and demonic that we don't even know it.

You can't go to the grocery store; you can't go out to eat; you can't watch a TV show or a movie; you can't listen to music; you can't buy shoes; you can't watch a football, baseball, or basketball game; you can't do a thing without the demonic, Satanic realm right in your face, and most of you don't even know it.

Most of you walk around supporting it and don't even know it.

The Devil is having a heyday with the church, laughing at us. We're a laughingstock.

So, what are we going to do about it?

When you know who you are and you know who you belong to, and you know the power that's in you, you can change things.

But you can't just sit back and allow the Devil to have his way with you.

Do you remember when the people were trying to put that demon out?

- Paul, I know.
- Jesus, I know.
- But who are you?

Does God know who you are?

Then again, does the Devil know who you are?

Or does the Devil just let you do what you want because you suck, and you aren't doing anything to go against the system of the world?

I told you I'm blunt. I can't help it. But remember, I got beat up first. This came to me first. And this is not what I'm here for. I'm not here to beat you up; I'm here to elevate. I'm trying to let you know what is in you.

The church is getting defeated because we don't know the power that we have.

What do you think Kingdom means? Heaven?

Thy kingdom come, thy will be done in Earth.

- Where did you get dominion?
- Where is your dominion?
- Is it in Heaven?
- Is it when you die?

Your dominion is in the Earth. This is why the Devil is having a heyday.

God has sanctified and ordained you to have *Purpose to Impact*.

So again, where is the impact of the church today? What is our excuse?

Jeremiah 1:6

⁶ Then said I, Ah, Lord GOD! behold, I cannot speak: for I am a child.

Then said I. You see that?

When God created the Heaven and the Earth, what did he do?

- God said.

God has known, sanctified, and ordained Jeremiah to be a prophet.

But what did Jeremiah say?

Then Jeremiah said, with his own mouth, "I cannot speak."

This is the opposite of God's Word.

Does it remind you of anything?

What happened in the garden?

- God said if you eat this fruit, you shall surely die.

What did the serpent say?

- You shall not surely die.

And what did they put their faith and their belief in?

- The word of the serpent, which is the opposition of God's word.

So, here we go again. There is nothing new under the sun. What is going on has already happened. This is a repetitive cycle.

Every time you read the Bible, I promise you, you can go back to Genesis, and everything you're looking for will be there.

Here we clearly see that Jeremiah is speaking the opposite of God's word.

Jeremiah 1:7

⁷ But the LORD said unto Jeremiah, Say not, I am a child: for thou shalt go to all that I shall send thee, and whatsoever I command thee thou shalt speak.

So here is the correction and direction from God. What did God speak?

- God's Word will not return void.
- Whatever God speaks will be as He has spoken.

But when you open your mouth, because you are a speaking spirit, you can override what God said and do what you want to do because you have the power of choice.

Here is God lining Jeremiah back up with the original Word that was spoken.

Jeremiah 1:8

⁸ Be not afraid of their faces: for I am with thee to deliver thee, saith the LORD.

What is another word for afraid?

- Fear

You see how this works?

- Fear is the enemy of your purpose.

If you are already equipped and ordained to do something, what is the excuse for not doing anything other than fear?

You listen to a different source, with a different voice, speaking a different word. Maybe your girlfriend or boyfriend or your fake preacher. Blunt as it can be, it is what it is.

A lot of times people do things that benefit themselves.

Why do you think I say I give myself away?

The only purpose you have in life, outside of figuring out what your purpose is, is to know that it is for other people.

- It's not for you.
- It's not for you to showboat.
- It's not for you to look good.
- It's not for you to trophy up.

It's for you to help God's people with *Purpose to Impact*. That's it.

Jeremiah 1:9–10

⁹ Then the LORD put forth his hand, and touched Jeremiah's mouth. And the LORD said unto Jeremiah, Behold, I have put my words in your mouth.

This is a very powerful prayer that I pray for myself personally. Remember, God is no respecter of persons, which means if He placed His words in Jeremiah's mouth, then He will place them in your mouth too. What better way to be close to God than to be empowered with His words when you speak to His people, to make them free from the foolishness of this world?

¹⁰ See, I have this day set thee over the nations and over the kingdoms, to root out, and to pull down, and to destroy, and to throw down, to build, and to plant.

To do what?

- Remember the word we are focused on right now is "Impact."

Let's walk through this verse using this word:

- Root out to Impact.
- Destroy to Impact.
- Throw down to Impact.
- Build to Impact.
- Plant to Impact.

Hopefully you are following me here.

We are talking about the *Purpose to Impact*.

- God knows Jeremiah.
- God has sanctified Jeremiah.
- God has ordained Jeremiah.

Jeremiah is afraid and speaks the opposite of what he has been ordained to do.

- God corrects him and brings him back into position.
- God places His words into Jeremiah's mouth.
- God gives him *Purpose to Impact*.

This is the same *Purpose to Impact* that every person in the world has. I don't care if they worship the Devil or know nothing about God. We're all God's children. It rains on the just and the unjust.

Now, people worship the Devil because it's cooler than church. People do the opposite of God's Word because it has more *Impact* than the church. I'm speaking from a place I know, and I will leave it at that.

Ecclesiastes 3:1

¹ To everything there is a season, and a time to every purpose under heaven.

1. To everything there is a season.
2. To everything there is a time.

And it's all for what?

1. Purpose.

Everything happens for a specific reason, at a specific time, for a specific purpose.

- A specific season you were placed here to Impact.
- A time designated for you to Impact.

Everything, and I mean everything, even the stuff you don't like, happens for a specific reason, at a specific time, for a specific purpose.

So, you are here for a specific reason, at this specific time.

Your purpose is to take what God has ordained you to be and positively Impact the lives of God's people.

It is seriously that simple. We are instructed, commanded, sanctified, and ordained to do the same thing that Jeremiah was told to do.

You might not be a prophet, but you are something. What are you?

That's not my place to say. As a matter of fact, that isn't anybody's place to say.

Every person has an individual purpose that God put them here to do. Your life will never change in the direction of what you want it to be, with a Positive Impact, until you find out what that is.

Other people can't find it for you. What I'm doing right now is just throwing out a seed. There's only one teacher. I'm not your teacher.

Nobody wants you to know that, though.

- Preachers and Priests aren't your teachers.
- Ministers and Deacons aren't your teachers.
- Other people, with their thoughts and opinions, aren't your teachers.

There is only one teacher: the Holy Spirit.

Revelation and confirmation come by the Spirit of God.

People can drop seeds, reveal, and confirm. When it is happening, you already know it's not the person.

The person may be telling you something you have heard before — that's confirmation — or they may be the first one to tell you — that's revelation.

You might not listen, but if you don't, then you'll go around the corner or around the block and hear it again. You may even read a book like this, and it will resonate with something you have read before.

No doubt, some of you are reading information that you have previously heard, and this is confirmation.

The Holy Spirit is your teacher.

- Look past me.
- It is not about me.
- I give myself away.

This right here isn't even who I am.

- I know who I am.
- I know where I come from.
- I know who I belong to.

And it isn't this funky world and all the things of it.

While we try to be representatives of the Kingdom, we don't even know that the Kingdom is here, not in Heaven.

We sing the songs, "Can't wait till I get to Heaven by and by."

What about while you're here?

Do something beneficial and productive for God's people. Help God out — not that He needs your help. Because if you don't do it, somebody else will.

Somebody else will step up and do it.

Jeremiah 1:10

[10] See, I have this day set thee over the nations and over the kingdoms, to root out, and to pull down, and to destroy, and to throw down, to build, and to plant.

This is the direction that was given to Jeremiah.

Ecclesiastes 3: 1–8

[1] To everything there is a season, and a time to every purpose under the heaven:

[2] A time to be born, and a time to die; a time to plant, and a time to pluck up that which is planted;

³ A time to kill, and a time to heal; a time to break down, and a time to build up;

⁴ A time to weep, and a time to laugh; a time to mourn, and a time to dance;

⁵ A time to cast away stones, and a time to gather stones together; a time to embrace, and a time to refrain from embracing;

⁶ A time to get, and a time to lose; a time to keep, and a time to cast away;

⁷ A time to rend, and a time to sow; a time to keep silence, and a time to speak;

⁸ A time to love, and a time to hate; a time of war, and a time of peace.

The very thing that Jeremiah was told to do in Verse 10 of Jeremiah Chapter 1 is the same thing that Solomon is talking about in Ecclesiastes Chapter 3. The very same thing: Impact.

Many of the things that were just mentioned, for those who were paying attention, apply.

A time to cast away. A time to get rid of playing around, playing church. A time to do something different, something better.

We all play a part in the ultimate plan to overcome evil and darkness.

- *Purpose to Impact.*
- *Season and Time.*

Based on Ecclesiastes 3:1, there is a season and a **time limit** for your *Purpose to Impact*.

Let that marinate:

- There is a season.
- There is a time limit.

This means you can't just do whatever you want the whole time you are here because the situation for your life is already written.

If you don't align with that situation, other things will happen.

Again, there's a season and a time limit for your *Purpose to Impact*.

What impact are you going to have on the lives of God's people while you're still here?

That's the easiest way to put it.

Luke 13:6–9

⁶ Jesus spake also this parable. A certain man had a fig tree planted in his vineyard; and this certain man came and sought fruit thereon, and found none.

⁷ Then said this man unto the person working, the dresser of the vineyard, Behold, these three years I come seeking fruit on this fig tree, and I found none: cut it down; why cumbereth it the ground?

⁸ And the man working answering said unto him, Lord, let it alone this year also, till I shall dig about it, fertilize it:

⁹ And if it bear fruit, well: and if not, then after that thou shalt cut it down.

Jesus spoke in many parables, and we clearly don't understand many of them.

A certain man came seeking fruit on his tree in its season and found nothing.

So, let's replace the word "fruit." A certain man came looking for Impact and found nothing.

Then said the man unto the man working, behold these three years.

What's three years? That's time, isn't it?

The fig tree is in season, but it's out of season.

It's been three years' time that I've been looking for figs on this fig tree, and I have not found any figs on this tree.

The man says, give it some time. Let me dig about it, let me fertilize it, and let me see what I can do. He is basically saying to check back next season.

So, here is my question for you:

Does God have to keep checking back next season?

If you even have the next season.

Understand that this is not a game, and this is not me. I'm just being real with you.

Why do you think I'm writing this chapter?

God called me when I was a child, and I went the opposite way.

- I don't want to do it.
- I don't want to be here.

I want to do what I want to do, how I want to do it. This is cool.

And the sad thing is, it still looks cool to some people right now.

Your fruit represents your Positive Impact on God's people.

What is the purpose of a fig tree?

- To bear figs.

What is the purpose of an apple tree?

- To bear apples.

What Impact does the fig tree or the apple tree have on the world if it doesn't provide any fruit?

- None.

The purpose of the fig tree is figs. If there are no figs, it has no purpose.

What is the Impact of the fig tree if it doesn't produce any figs?

- None.

What's the purpose of a lawn mower?

- To cut grass.

But if it's sitting in a garage, catching dust, what Impact is it having other than getting in your way?

- None.

Are you that lawn mower?

What's the purpose of a car?

- To drive.

If the car doesn't ever go anywhere because you never put the keys in the ignition to crank it up and go, what's its Impact, other than sitting in your driveway or garage, taking up space?

- None.

What's the point of God giving you purpose if you have no Impact?

Where is your fruit?

Don't allow the Devil to make you feel like you have Impact when you truly don't, especially when you know you aren't doing anything beneficial or productive with the talents that God has given you.

Sitting around playing church will not suffice in the end.

Are you maximizing your *Purpose to Impact*, in your season, in your time?

- *Purpose to Impact.*
- *Season and Time.*

Let's go to a place in the Bible where it makes a little bit more sense and talk about purpose with somebody who holds more importance for most people.

Mark 11:11–14

[11] And Jesus entered into Jerusalem, and into the temple: and when Jesus had looked round about upon all things, and now the eventide was come, Jesus went out unto Bethany with the twelve.

[12] And on the morrow, when they were come from Bethany, Jesus was hungry:

[13] And seeing a fig tree afar off having leaves, Jesus came, if haply He might find anything thereon: and when Jesus came to it, He found nothing but leaves; for the time of figs was not yet.

¹⁴ And Jesus answered and said unto the fig tree, No man eat fruit of you hereafter forever. And Jesus' disciples heard it.

- Jesus was hungry.
- Jesus saw a fig tree with leaves.
- Jesus was happy to find some fruit.
- Jesus only found leaves.
- Jesus answers the tree that has leaves but no fruit.

Jesus is hungry, and He sees a fig tree far off. I can just see Jesus now. He is hungry, skipping, and happy. The tree is solid, with green leaves, nice bark, and big branches.

But when Jesus gets there, there isn't anything but leaves.

This is just like a lot of people's praise, prayer time, Bible study, and church attendance — real church attendance, not the building. You know, your personal relationship with God, so you can become one with God.

Let's replace the word "fruit with Impact." Jesus came by to see you. In the process of coming by to see you, Jesus was looking for some Impact.

You looked good, you were dressed well, your Bible was heavy, and it was in all the right places while you were walking. Your shoes were shiny, you sounded and looked the part, but when Jesus looked for Impact, he found none.

We must stop playing. This is real. We are at war.

Turn on your TV, your radio, and even the commercials; you can't even buy cereal, a drink, or food from the grocery store without demonic, Satanic emblems and energy all in your face.

How long will you be a beautiful tree with strong roots, nice bark, great branches, and bright green leaves, with no fruit and no Impact?

How long will you be full of God-given purpose with no productive Impact on God's people?

When Jesus sees you, what does He see?

And this is not judgmental, because only you know what Jesus sees.

You can pretend to be something you're not in the world all day.

I don't care about that. I care about where you go and how many people you can help get there, and I care about the Impact. I don't care about your personal situation. That's your business.

But is what you show us real? Because you can't hide from God.

Is what you show in public and in the church real, or is your light shining only in the church building?

Can I tell the difference between you and the world?

Of course, this goes for me, too. I am not exempt from the words that I am writing.

Can you see, feel, or notice a difference between the Devil and you?

When Jesus walks by, does he see a Pharisee and a Sadducee who's playing the part, or does he see somebody whose giving themselves away?

Some of you know the story of the talents.

"Talents" is a good word to illustrate the point — although it's not talent, it's money.

But you can use it like that, and you can also replace it with the word "Impact."

The man gave five talents to one. He gave two talents to another. And then he gave one talent. The person with five talents had Impact and got five more. The person with two had Impact and got two more. But the person with one — I want you to understand why it's a problem.

This is Jesus telling another parable. Who do you think Jesus is talking about?

Matthew 25:14–15

¹⁴ For the kingdom of heaven is as a man travelling into a far country, who called his own servants, and delivered unto them his goods.

¹⁵ And unto one he gave five talents, to another two, and to another one; to every man according to his several ability; and straightway took his journey.

This is the part I want you to get. Pay attention to this: several ability, which means unto their own ability. Their ability is equivalent to the *Purpose to Impact*.

The story may not make sense if you don't understand that part. That is a very specific verse with very specific verbiage. God did not give you something that you could not do.

Going back to what God told Jeremiah:

- He knew you.
- He sanctified you.
- He ordained you.
- He gave you *Purpose to Impact*.

So, with that *Purpose to Impact*, God gave you a talent. You are supposed to take that talent and go do something with it, so you can help somebody else.

- The one with five went and got five. Good Impact.
- The one with two went and got two. Good Impact.

But what happened to the one who received one talent?

Matthew 25:25

²⁵ And I was afraid, and went and hid thy talent in the earth: lo, there thou hast that is thine.

What is another word for "afraid"?

- Fear

This gives us a basic idea of why.

And what did he do with his talent?

- Hid it in the earth.

God blessed him with Impact and the *Purpose to Impact* God's people, and what he decided to do with that *Purpose to Impact* was to go hide it in the ground.

How many of us are hiding our God-given *Purpose to Impact* in the ground?

Matthew 25:26

²⁶ His Lord answered and said unto him, Thou wicked and slothful servant, thou knewest that I reap where I sowed not, and gather where I have not strawed:

This gives us an idea of what fear does to you. Fear, which is the opposition of God's word, makes you wicked, lazy, and — as stated in Verse 30 — unprofitable.

You've been given the ability to Impact, but out of fear, you decided, "I'm not going to do anything with what God gave me. I'm scared. I don't know what to do." Fear.

Does God give the spirit of fear?

- No.

Who gives the spirit of fear?

- The Devil.

I hope you are following me. I know it may seem as if we are going in circles and talking about the same thing, but I need you to see it in the Bible. I am showing you, word for word, what's what and why the *Purpose to Impact* is so important.

Fear brings wickedness and laziness, and it makes you unprofitable.

What are you going to do with the talent that God gave you if you are wicked, lazy, and unprofitable?

- The same thing this guy did: absolutely nothing.

Matthew 25:28-29

[28] Take therefore the talent from him, and give it unto him which hath ten talents.

[29] For unto every one that hath shall be given, and he shall have abundance: but from him that hath not shall be taken away even that which he hath.

Take the talent or Impact from him — the Impact that I gave him before he was ever born. Take that from him and give it to this person over here who's making things happen. Basically, take his *Purpose to Impact*.

For unto everyone that has shall be given, and he shall have abundance. But from him that has not — the person who had the talent but didn't do anything about it — take it and give it to somebody who is impacting lives and utilizing *Purpose to Impact*. That's the Word.

There's Negative Impact, and there's Positive Impact. Now, I do things the way I do them on purpose because I don't want any excuses. Excuses irritate me, and I guarantee you if they irritate me, they irritate God.

I verify in the Old Testament and the New Testament. I have given you example after example so that you understand your Impact means something.

You have a power within you to do something that God is allowing only you to do. There is something that God put you here specifically to do.

- Nobody can do what God put me here to do.
- Nobody can do what God put you here to do.

It's simple. We make stuff so difficult.

What am I supposed to do with myself?

- Am I supposed to preach?
- Am I supposed to sit?
- Am I supposed to pray?
- Am I supposed to usher?
- Am I supposed to play the keyboard or the bass?

What did God ordain you to do?

- Do what God told you to do.

Just make the effort to do something. Doing nothing must not be an option.

God is the God of the living, not of the dead. People who do nothing are dead.

Read Matthew 25:31–46

Matthew 25:31–34

³¹ When the Son of man shall come in his glory, and all the holy angels with him, then shall he sit upon the throne of his glory:

³² And before him shall be gathered all nations: and he shall separate them one from another, as a shepherd divides his sheep from the goats:

³³ And he shall set the sheep on his right hand, but the goats on the left.

³⁴ Then shall the King say unto them on his right hand, Come, you blessed of my Father, inherit the kingdom prepared for you from the foundation of the world:

Like I said before, I can write about this until Jesus comes back.

- You were known before you were here.
- Your purpose was already here, too.
- The Kingdom prepared for you from the foundation of the world.

What is the word we are highlighting?

- Impact.

This is *Purpose to Impact* in a positive manner.

Matthew 25:35–36

- I was hungry, and you gave me meat. Impact.
- I was thirsty, and you gave me a drink. Impact.
- I was a stranger, and you took me in. Impact.
- I was naked, and you clothed me. Impact.
- I was sick, and you visited me. Impact.
- I was in prison, and you came to me. Impact.

Matthew 25:37–39

Then shall the righteous answer him. I'm going to shorten this up, so be sure to read this for yourself.

- When did we do that, God?
- When did we feed you when you were hungry?
- When did we get you something to drink?
- When did we clothe you?
- When did we do all these things?

Matthew 25:40

[40] And the King shall answer and say unto them, Verily I say unto you, Inasmuch as ye have done it unto one of the least of these my brethren, ye have done it unto me.

Matthew 25:34 is the result:

[34] Then shall the King say unto them on his right hand, Come, ye blessed of my Father, inherit the kingdom prepared for you from the foundation of the world:

The *Purpose to Impact* is for God's people. It's not for yourself. Everything God gave you is for someone else, so in the process of doing these things, you have a Positive Impact on others.

The Bible tells us when you lend to the poor, it's as if you lend unto the Lord, and the Lord shall repay.

This verse is not very different. When you do unto God's people and Impact those people's lives, then you are doing it as unto God. That's the positive.

Here's the negative, which is pretty much everything in opposition.

Matthew 25:42–43

- I was hungry, and you didn't give me any meat. No Impact.
- I was thirsty, and you didn't give me a drink. No Impact.
- I was a stranger, and you didn't take me in. No Impact.
- I was naked, and you didn't clothe me. No Impact.
- I was sick, and you didn't visit me. No Impact.
- I was in prison, and you didn't come to me. No Impact.

Matthew 25:44

Then they shall answer him and ask the same questions that the righteous have asked him. Be sure to read this for yourself.

- When did we not do that, God?
- When did we not feed you when you were hungry?
- When did we not get you something to drink?
- When did we not clothe you?
- When did we not do all these things?

Matthew 25:45

[45] Then shall he answer them, saying, Verily I say unto you, Inasmuch as ye did it not do it to the least of these, you didn't do it to me.

Matthew 25:41 is the result.

[41] Then shall he say also unto them on the left hand, Depart from me, ye cursed, into everlasting fire, prepared for the devil and his angels:

So, you have the positive and you have the negative, which means Impact works both ways.

- Devil worshippers have Impact.
- Gangs have Impact.
- Thieves have Impact.
- Murderers have Impact.

The world is full of Impact, but which side are you going to be on?

We must have a Positive Impact on the lives of God's people to change their mentality and mindset, to truly make them free from the distractions, tricks, and traps of this world by eliminating fear and the contradiction of God's word.

We have already been given *Purpose to Impact* the lives of God's people with the instructions to *Seek and to Save* that which was lost and bring the lost back home.

- That means when you're with the 99 people in church, and one person is lost, you leave the 99 for the one.
- That means when you're with 99 healthy people, and one person is sick, you go to the one who is sick.
- That means you see that person who is hungry and thirsty and naked and has nowhere to stay, you leave the 99, and go after that one.

You leave your comfort, and you go and seek out that one who needs God the most.

This is a lot deeper than I can convey here because it is very easy to sit around in comfort. It is easy to become comfortable.

Even when you think you're having a Positive Impact, it could be nothing but the chair.

Purpose to Impact

It's got to be something bigger and something better.

- We must speak out.
- We must lead.
- We must act.
- We must Impact.

Ask yourself these three simple questions:

1. Are you maximizing your Purpose to Impact?
2. Is this your season?
3. Is there a better time than right now?

Notes:

_____

_____

_____

_____

_____

_____

_____

_____

_____

_____

_____

Notes:

Conclusion

I sincerely pray that this book reaches the heart and mind of every individual who reads it, but unfortunately discernment and my lack of naivety have prepared me for the pushback and the mentality of "in one ear and out the other" that haunts the majority.

I have been preaching *The True Power of Unity* since 2017 and the *Purpose to Impact* since 2023, and it is as if I am talking to myself. Even worse, there are times it is accepted and appreciated in the moment, but does not find the Good Ground, so it ends up on the Wayside, Thorns, and/or Stony Ground.

We spend way too much time being religious and traditional rather than applying the tools that God has given us to make real change. We talk a good game, but our hearts are far away from the goals that matter to us and our families the most.

People are choosing:

- Religion rather than building a relationship.
- To be entertained rather than educated.
- Darkness rather than light.
- The lie rather than the Truth.
- What is fake rather than what is real.
- Division rather than unity.
- The World's System rather than the Kingdom of God.

When you understand that we do not fight against flesh and blood but against principalities, it becomes easier to see the demonic and Satanic attacks you face every day.

- You must understand *The True Power of Unity.*
- You must find your *Purpose to Impact.*

God has ordained and sanctified you to be an Ambassador of the Kingdom and equipped you with what you need to be successful at seeking to save that which is lost and bringing people back to their Father's house where they belong.

Life would be so much simpler if we just followed the blueprint provided in The Acts of the Apostles.

The number one reason churches are suffering today is that they lack Acts.

The True Power of Unity begins with you becoming one unit, united with God. This enables you to be in a position where nothing will be withheld from you.

When we work together in unison to fulfill Kingdom Purpose, we exemplify the Power of God in an amazing way that empowers and encourages others to see the Father, Son, and Spirit within us.

You must know who you are, who you belong to, and what you stand for, or you may fall for anything.

Conclusion

God is God, and He has gifted you to be a great representation and reflection of Him for the world to see.

Choose you on this day whom you will serve.

The True Power of Unity is within you,

Sincerely and respectfully,

Brian P. Lucas

BRIAN P. LUCAS
Kingdom Ambassador

Kingdom Ambassador: An official representative sent by God to the World's System to promote and exemplify the *Kingdom* and the *Culture of the Kingdom* in word and action, to teach a *Kingdom Mentality* and *Kingdom Mindset* to fulfill purpose — *Kingdom Purpose*!

Why Jesus?

Why Did Jesus Come? Luke 19:10 / John 10:10

For the Son of man [Jesus] is come to seek and to save that which was lost.

The thief comes not, but for to steal, and to kill, and to destroy: I [Jesus] am come that they might have life, and that they might have [life] more abundantly.

Why Do I Need Jesus? Matthew 28:18 / John 14:6
John 10:9

And Jesus came and spake unto them, saying, All power is given unto [Jesus] in heaven and in earth.

Jesus saith unto him, I am the way, the truth, and the life: no person comes unto the Father [God], but by [Jesus].

I [Jesus] am the door: by [Jesus] if any [person] enters in, [that person] shall be saved, and shall go in and out, and find pasture.

Jesus or the World? Mark 8:35–37

For whosoever will save their life shall lose their life; but whosoever shall lose their life for [Jesus] sake and the gospel's, the same shall save their life. For what shall it profit a [person], if they shall gain the whole world, and lose their own soul?

Salvation

For those of you who are not saved, simply read the verses below and *Make It Personal* by adding your name in the spaces provided. You will see how simple it is to receive the greatest gift that God has provided you since the fall of man.

Luke 19:10

For the Son of man [Jesus] has come to seek and to save _____ which was lost.

Romans 10:9–10

That if _____ shalt confess with _____'s mouth the Lord Jesus, and shalt believe in _____'s heart that God has raised [Jesus] from the dead, _____ shalt be saved. For with the heart _____ believes unto righteousness; and with _____'s mouth confession is made unto salvation.

John 3: 16–18

For God so loved _____, that [God] gave his only begotten Son [Jesus] that if _____ believes in [Jesus] _____ should not perish but have everlasting life. For God did not send his Son [Jesus] into the world to condemn _____; but that _____ through [Jesus] might be saved. If _____ believes on [Jesus] _____ is not condemned: but if _____ does not believe [in Jesus] then _____ is condemned already, because _____ has not believed in the name of [Jesus] the only begotten Son of God.

Please realize that all the things people have conditioned and brainwashed us to think about salvation are nowhere to be found in these verses.

We don't need religion, rules, regulations, traditions of men, priests, sprinkles of water, Hail Marys, incense, statues, animals, yoga, science, the universe, or any of the other foolishness they use to control and enslave us and keep us ignorant of Truth.

God's Word is Truth, and every man a liar. This is yet another reason why it is extremely important for you study to show yourself approved and allow the Spirit of God (not man) to rightly divide the Word of Truth for you.

For those of you who are already saved, my prayer is that you understand your daily assignment to seek and save the lost and bring them back home to their Father's House. This is how you empower yourself and others to fulfill *Kingdom Purpose*.

About the Author

Most importantly, above anything and everything else, I believe in and I trust the God in Heaven, who is the God of the Bible. I believe in God the Father, Jesus the Christ, and the Holy Spirit. I believe that Jesus is the Son of God and that Jesus died on the cross for my sins, transgressions, and unrighteousness. I believe in the resurrection, that Jesus was raised from the dead and that Jesus now sits on the right hand of God the Father with all power in Heaven and on Earth. I respectfully believe without compromise, doubts, or any second thoughts that Jesus is the one and only way to God the Father and that Jesus is the one and only way to receive Salvation and Forgiveness by the Mercy and Grace of God.

Now, am I an angel, holier than thou, full of righteousness by my own power, religious, or perfect? No!

Frankly, if I were or if anyone else actually could be, then there would be no need for Jesus or a Savior, because we would just press our holiness button and save ourselves.

I am nothing without God; this book and everything else I possess belongs to God, so I refuse to compromise on my faith and belief in God.

I am but a lonely voice in the wilderness that has experienced my own personal road to Damascus and has been awakened to a glimpse of the truth that every human being searches for.

One great thing about truth is that it is always true. Whether it's coming from a doctor or a janitor, a multi-millionaire or someone living in poverty, someone driving a luxury car or someone riding a bicycle, a dope dealer on the corner or a preacher behind the pulpit, the truth is always the truth!

Truth in word will always resonate with those who are seeking it. My birds will know my feathers and flock with me, and the sheep I am responsible for will know my voice. I will resonate with them, and they will resonate with me.

I am that I am, not what the world tells me or attempts to market and advertise me to be.

My life forever changed when I came to the simple conclusion that the world owes me nothing and that I am not entitled to anything outside of my faith that I have not worked for or willed my way.

I now understand the importance of having eyes to see and ears to hear, which enable me to see through the deception the world consistently promotes to the walking blind, who have their eyes wide shut.

I strongly believe that ethics, morals, and character still mean something today, no matter what this new world is shoving down our throats!

I promote unity over division, I support equality over slavery, and I respect hard work and not laziness.

Mentality and mindset are key: stand for something, or you will fall for anything!

About the Author

Here is my bio summed up:

I once was lost, but now I am found; I once was blind, but now I see.

My only goal and purpose in life is to open the eyes of as many people as possible while I am still here, so that each day I am hopefully putting a smile on God's face.

Every day, I want to imagine God saying, "Well done, good and faithful servant."

I am that I am because of who Jesus is.

I have what I have because of what Jesus has.

I can do what I do because of what Jesus did for me on the cross.

I am nothing without Jesus!

Every experience and accomplishment I am blessed to possess and all my joy come from the aforementioned.

Sincerely and respectfully,

Brian P. Lucas
BRIAN P. LUCAS

Author: Brian P. Lucas

Discover the quickest, easiest, most convenient way to reach your personal goals in life, by living on your own terms and by your own definitions and ultimately determining your own personal definition of perfection. If you are ready to find out who you really are and begin to live by your own definitions, and you are truly interested in succeeding and utilizing a system that's proven to work, this may be the book for you.

Author: Brian P. Lucas

Each and every day, seeds are being planted, and it is up to us to determine exactly how each seed will take root and manifest in our personal lives. The Harvest is dictated by the ground in which the seed is planted. If the ground is good, then the Harvest has the potential to be great. We must empower the Good Ground in our lives to produce a Great Harvest for our families and future generations to come.

Author: Brian P. Lucas

Back to the Garden shines light in the darkness and provides the only Truth that will make you free from the rules, regulations, religion, and the traditions of men.

You must empower the *Kingdom of God* which is within you to eliminate the brainwashing and conditioning influences of the World's System.

You must *Know Who You Are* to fulfill *Kingdom Purpose*.

Author: Brian P. Lucas

Simply Believe highlights John's Walk with Jesus in an easy-to-read format with a purposely repetitive verse-by-verse breakdown.

Brian P. Lucas provides you with a direct and engaging commentary to empower you to have a greater understanding of The Gospel According to St. John.

God is Love, and God loves you.

Discover the gift of Truth that only God will provide, and Simply Believe.

Author: Brian P. Lucas

God has a specific message for every one of us, if we simply have the ears to hear His voice when He speaks.

Do not be fooled by the World's System and the religious puppets who attempt to dictate and deteriorate the message that God has for you.

People are searching for the Truth because it is only the Truth that brings real freedom.

We must understand God's Message to Teach, Preach, and Heal.

Author: Brian P. Lucas

Honesty opens our eyes to see *Truth*, and the *Truth* brings us revelation and confirmation that forces us to get out of our own comfort zones.

Elevation, growth, and development are key to building successful relationships, and we must be knowledgeable of one another's motives in the process.

We must make it a point to eliminate the toxic relationships in our lives and find our purpose.

Author: Brian P. Lucas

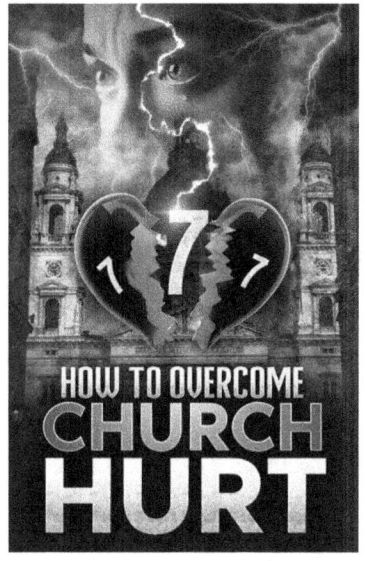

Church Hurt is real, and it empowers division to destroy unity.

Many people have turned away from God because of the hurt, pain, abuse, and rejection of Man. Whether it be *condemnation, discrimination,* and *disrespect,* or whispers, stares, pointed fingers, mockery, and *gossip,* we must not allow ourselves to be distracted.

You cannot allow the ignorance and failures of others to dictate your personal relationship with God. Man is *not* God and God is *not* Man. Man will fail you, but God will *never* fail you, leave you, or forsake you.

The lack of *biblical leadership* in the church has destroyed many people's walk with God because they mistakenly base their value of God on the actions of Man. We spend too much time and energy focused on Man, and the rules, regulations, and traditions of men, which are nothing more than purposeful distractions to keep us from experiencing God's best.

Church Hurt is a tool that Satan uses to keep you from trusting God.

Knowing *How to Overcome Church Hurt* is extremely important for your elevation, growth, and development.

www.ingramcontent.com/pod-product-compliance
Lightning Source LLC
Chambersburg PA
CBHW070919080526
44589CB00013B/1365